THE **Aftermath** OF THE **French Defeat** in Vietnam

MARK E. CUNNINGHAM AND LAWRENCE J. ZWIER

TWENTY-FIRST CENTURY BOOKS   MINNEAPOLIS

Consultant: Jim Arnold, military historian

The image on the jacket and cover shows French army paratroopers searching a wooded area near Dien Bien Phu, Vietnam, during war operations against Viet Minh forces in 1954. (Photo © AP Photo).

Twenty-First Century Books
A division of Lerner Publishing Group, Inc.
241 First Avenue North
Minneapolis, MN 55401 U.S.A.

Website address: www.lernerbooks.com

Library of Congress Cataloging-in-Publication Data

Cunningham, Mark E.
    The aftermath of the French defeat in Vietnam / Mark Cunningham and Lawrence J. Zwier.
      p.   cm. — (Aftermath of history)
    Includes bibliographical references and index.
    ISBN 978-0-8225-9093-4 (lib. bdg. : alk. paper)
    1. Dien Bien Phu, Battle of, Dien Bien Phu, Vietnam, 1954—Juvenile literature. 2. France. Armée—History—20th century—Juvenile literature. 3. Vietnam—History—1945–1975—Juvenile literature. 4. Vietnam—Politics and government—1945–1975—Juvenile literature. 5. France—Colonies—Asia—Juvenile literature. 6. Vietnam War, 1961–1975—Causes—Juvenile literature. I. Zwier, Lawrence J. II. Title.
DS553.3.D5C86 2009
959.704'1—dc22   2008051924

Manufactured in the United States of America
1 2 3 4 5 6 — BP — 14 13 12 11 10 09

Contents

The End of the Beginning

THE DATE IS NOVEMBER 20, 1953. In a beautiful highland valley, the sun has burned off the morning mist. Vietnamese villagers are tending their livestock, toting buckets of water, and working the rice fields as their ancestors have done for a thousand years. Those who hold power in their land—soldiers of the Viet Minh movement—are in the valley, eyeing a lone aircraft that circles far overhead. Not long before, the soldiers chased a French army from the hill country, but France still holds the lowlands that are home to most Vietnamese people. For seven years, the Viet Minh have been fighting to force the French out of Vietnam, but the French will leave only on their own terms.

From the distant hills and mountains that rim the wide valley comes the sound of engines. The villagers look up. Aircraft appear in formation and level off. Out tumble tiny figures. A streamer of white cloth ripples and blossoms above each figure. The sky fills with parachutes. Suspended beneath their canopies, the figures approach the ground, hit, and roll. Men in camouflage uniforms get up, detach themselves from their parachutes, and ready their weapons.

The Viet Minh react quickly, shooting at the arriving paratroopers and launching mortar rounds among them, but the aggressive paratroopers soon push the Viet Minh back. The "paras" are the elite fighters of the French army, but they are far from France. Their battlefield on this day is Vietnam, which France has dominated since the mid-1800s.

On this day, the beautiful valley in a far corner of Vietnam will become an arena for a dramatic act in an agonizing struggle between colonizer and colonized. The battle in the valley will not be a closing act, however. It ends one fight—and begins another.

ELITE FRENCH PARATROOPERS DESCENDED ON DIEN BIEN PHU IN VIETNAM NOVEMBER 20, 1953, FOR A FINAL BATTLE WITH THE VIET MINH.

CHAPTER 1

Its Own Nation

VIETNAM IS A NARROW COUNTRY in Southeast Asia. Just over 1,000 miles (1,609 kilometers) long from north to south, the nation contains a long north-south mountain chain, with peaks rising to 10,000 feet (3,048 meters). To the east of the mountains, coastal lowlands border the South China Sea. The Vietnamese people mainly live in the fertile lowlands, where the coastal plain broadens out in the Red River delta in the North and the Mekong River delta in the South.

Vietnam is part of a larger region called Indochina. In addition to Vietnam, Indochina includes the nations of Burma (also called Myanmar), Thailand, Cambodia, and Laos, as well as West Malaysia. Indochina is situated between two of the most important civilizations in Asia—China and India. For thousands of years, these states influenced the people of Indochina and shaped their history and culture.

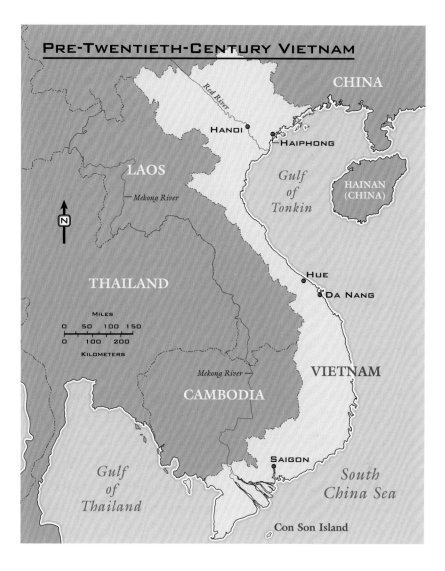

PRE-TWENTIETH-CENTURY VIETNAM

CHINA

Red River

HANOI

HAIPHONG

LAOS

Gulf
of
Tonkin

HAINAN
(CHINA)

Mekong River

N

THAILAND

HUE

DA NANG

MILES

0   50   100 150

0   100   200

KILOMETERS

VIETNAM

Mekong River

CAMBODIA

SAIGON

Gulf
of
Thailand

South
China Sea

Con Son Island

THE VIETNAMESE

People have lived in Indochina since prehistoric times. The first in-
habitants lived by gathering wild plants and hunting. By about 7000
B.C., people in Indochina had begun to farm. The first distinctive

Vietnamese ethnic group emerged in the Red River area of northern Vietnam. People there made their living by growing rice in the lowlands. Vietnam's mountain areas were home to a number of non-Vietnamese ethnic groups.

In 207 B.C., Chinese rulers took control of Vietnam. The Chinese at first ruled indirectly, allowing Vietnamese nobles to govern in Vietnam. Later, the Chinese sent their own officials to rule the area directly. These officials, called mandarins, were highly educated and earned their jobs through competitive examinations.

Most ordinary Vietnamese people were farmers who lived in rural villages. The family was the all-important foundation of Vietnamese society. People displayed loyalty to their families, their villages, and ultimately to their rulers. Those with authority were expected to use their power virtuously, and those under them were expected to obey and respect that authority.

In addition to their governance system, the Chinese spread their spiritual beliefs to Vietnam. From the Chinese, the Vietnamese learned about the teachings of Confucius, an ancient Chinese philosopher, and Buddha, a religious teacher from India.

The Vietnamese adopted many features of Chinese culture but never lost a sense of their own identity or a wish for independence. Several times, the Vietnamese rebelled against Chinese rule. A revolt in 939, against a weak Chinese ruler, succeeded in driving the Chinese out of Vietnam. After that, the Vietnamese ruled their own nation.

Vietnamese rulers established the kingdom of Dai Viet in the Red River area of the North and oversaw expansion of their kingdom southward. In so doing, they came into conflict with the Champa people of central Vietnam, a group that had been heavily influenced by India.

Conflict with China continued. Led by a dynasty (ruling family) called the Tran, the Vietnamese defeated invading Chinese armies in the thirteenth and fourteenth centuries. After another leader overthrew the Tran in 1400, China's powerful Ming dynasty invaded Vietnam. Under Le Loi, the Vietnamese eventually drove out the Chinese. Le Loi then proclaimed himself emperor.

EAST MEETS WEST

For thousands of years, the people of Asia had little contact with Westerners, save for a few European adventurers such as Marco Polo. But trade increased greatly when Portuguese ships arrived in India in 1498. Within a few decades, the Portuguese dominated trade in southern Asia. Portuguese and other European traders sought valuable Asian goods, such as spices and silk. Portugal did business through coastal outposts such as Goa in India, Melaka on the Malay Peninsula, and Macao in southeastern China.

To protect access to trade, the Europeans often made alliances with local Asian rulers. If anyone interfered with their trade, the Europeans could be ruthless. They did not hesitate to use seaborne firepower to protect their trade networks.

Portuguese traders arrived in Vietnam in 1516. They were followed a decade later by Portuguese missionaries, religious workers who tried to teach Vietnamese people about Christianity. Traders and missionaries set up a small outpost near the Vietnamese town of Da Nang. Vietnam's rulers tolerated the Portuguese merchants, but the Portuguese gradually lost interest in Vietnam. They had more profitable trade connections elsewhere in Asia.

Meanwhile, Vietnamese rulers kept moving south. They conquered

Champa territory and pushed a group called the Khmer from the Mekong Delta. By the 1500s, the Le dynasty was weakening. It lost control in the North and struggled to regain it. By the 1600s, the real powers in Vietnam were the Nguyen family in the South and the Trinh family in the North. The Le emperors were figureheads—or symbolic rulers.

By this time, more Europeans had arrived in Vietnam. In addition to Portuguese missionaries, French missionaries came to teach Vietnamese people about Catholicism. One of them was Alexandre de Rhodes. During two stays in Vietnam, from 1619 to 1630 and 1640 to 1646, he converted thousands of Vietnamese to Catholicism (a major branch of Christianity). Earlier, Portuguese missionaries had developed a Vietnamese alphabet using modified Latin characters (used to write English and other European languages). Rhodes perfected this alphabet, which became the basis for modern Vietnamese writing.

Rhodes wrote about his experiences in Vietnam, and his writings created interest among other French people. Shortly after, French people set up a missionary society in Vietnam. A firm called the French East India Company, based in India, also promoted French trade and increased French involvement in Asia.

Allies

In 1772 rebels from the Tay Son region of Vietnam overthrew the Nguyen and Trinh families. The rebels then rallied the Vietnamese to defeat another Chinese invasion in 1788.

Nguyen Anh, a prince of the defeated Nguyen family, fled to an island near Cambodia, where he met a French missionary-adventurer named Pierre Pigneau de Béhaine. Pigneau was on the island training Asian-born missionaries. He agreed to help the young prince reassert his clan's control of southern Vietnam.

Accompanied by Nguyen's young son, Pigneau went all the way to France and met with King Louis XVI, who promised French military assistance and weapons for Nguyen Anh. In exchange, Nguyen Anh agreed to let the French use the port of Da Nang and to control Con Son Island, a large island off southeastern Vietnam. He also gave special trading privileges for the French.

But by the time Pigneau

FRENCH MISSIONARY PIERRE PIGNEAU DE BÉHAINE HELPED NGUYEN ANH GAIN CONTROL OF VIETNAM.

arrived at a French post in India to mount an expedition to help Nguyen Anh, official French support had collapsed. So Pigneau raised a private expedition that helped Nguyen Anh crush the Tay Son rebels. Nguyen Anh declared himself emperor of all Vietnam in 1802. Calling himself Emperor Gia Long, he established his seat of government at Hue in central Vietnam.

By this time, Vietnam had largely attained its modern shape and size. It had three distinct regions: the North, centered on the city of Hanoi and the nearby Red River delta; a central region around the new imperial capital at Hue; and the southern region with the Mekong Delta and the city of Saigon. The Vietnamese by then also shared a distinctive national culture and a strong sense of being one nation. They wanted to live under their own rulers.

CHAPTER 2

Empires

IN EUROPE THE INDUSTRIAL REVOLUTION of the late eighteenth and nineteenth centuries brought wealth and power to many parts of the continent. The newly industrialized nations of Europe had the manufacturing capacity and the cash to produce deadly weapons for their increasingly effective military forces. They used military power to expand their trade empires and to take over resource-rich territories in Asia and Africa.

Britain and France used their naval fleets, their advanced military organization, and their industrial strength ruthlessly. They pressured China and Japan to trade with them. They forced direct or indirect rule on most of India and much of Southeast Asia.

To the northeast, Russia pushed across Siberia and seized territories claimed by China. In Southeast Asia, the Dutch extended their rule over Indonesia, a declining Spain held on to the Philippines, and

Portugal maintained old enclaves such as Macao and East Timor. Although they sometimes cooperated when their interests coincided, the strong powers often competed to control Asia and Africa for their own benefit.

Once again, trade and religion intertwined. As European empires expanded, many people in Europe believed it was their duty to extend Christianity to the peoples of Asia and Africa. They looked down upon traditional Asian religions such as Buddhism. By spreading Christianity, they believed, they would save people's souls and bring "civilization" to less advanced nations.

FRIENDSHIP YOU CAN'T REFUSE

With a powerful mix of motives—both economic and spiritual—many Europeans thought that empire building was a good idea. Citizens of Western countries felt pride in their nations' economic and military strength and felt competitive toward other European nations. They also believed they were helping the nations they colonized and conquered. Colonized nations dared not refuse this "help." If they rejected European trade, insulted the flag of a European nation, or opposed the spread of Christianity, they risked harsh reprisals.

Vietnam's rulers took this risk. Although the French had helped the Nguyen dynasty gain power in 1802, they worried that a Western presence in their nation would threaten their hard-won independence. So the Vietnamese expelled most French advisers. They persecuted and sometimes executed French missionaries and Vietnamese converts to Catholicism. By doing so, however, they provided an excuse for a French takeover of Vietnam.

THE FRENCH HEAVILY INFLUENCED VIETNAMESE CULTURE. SOME VIETNAMESE CHILDREN, SUCH AS THESE IN THE LATE 1800S, ATTENDED CATHOLIC SCHOOLS ESTABLISHED BY FRENCH PRIESTS.

Claiming they had to protect French missionaries in Asia, the French sent a fleet to Vietnam. In March 1847, the ships arrived at Da Nang to rescue a French priest who was reportedly being held captive. The French fleet shelled the harbor to warn the Vietnamese against abusing French missionaries and as a show of strength. (The captive priest had already been released.)

Worried that missionaries were an advance guard for another French invasion, Emperor Tu Duc ordered another crackdown on Vietnamese Catholics and foreign priests in 1851. His troops executed a few more missionaries. This was the last straw for the French, who began plans to seize Vietnamese ports and force French rule on Vietnam.

FRANCE RULES

With the approval of France's strongman ruler, Napoléon III, French forces invaded, seizing Da Nang in August 1858. The French then shifted their focus to Saigon and the surrounding area. In 1862 the French forced Emperor Tu Duc to sign a treaty that gave France control of much of southern Vietnam, an area known as Cochin China. The French first built up their position in the South. Then, in a series of campaigns, French forces overcame resistance in the rest of Vietnam. By the mid-1880s, the French had taken over central and northern Vietnam (known as Annam and Tonkin, respectively). The French also brought Cambodia and Laos under their rule.

At the end of the nineteenth century, France governed Annam, Tonkin, Laos, and Cambodia as protectorates. Under this arrangement, these areas were supposed to have their own governments and local rulers, but they could do little without French approval. French officials ruled Cochin China more directly. In theory, France was merely supposed to protect the Indochinese nations from whatever problems they could not handle themselves. In practice, the governments were operated by French people, along French lines, and largely for French benefit. French people held all positions of authority in police departments, railways, and city and rural government. They conducted most business in French.

FRANCE'S CIVILIZING MISSION

France claimed to be on a "civilizing mission" to help the lands it colonized, but this claim rang hollow in Vietnam. The French offered a French-style education to a small Vietnamese elite, while most Vietnamese remained uneducated. The French colonizers enjoyed modern medical care, while most Vietnamese had no modern care.

Vietnam had long been a major rice-growing area, and rice yields and exports increased in colonial times. Nevertheless, the economic conditions of Vietnam's rice-growing peasants—the majority of the population—steadily worsened. Increasingly, French-connected Vietnamese landlords took over productive land. Taxes and gouging by brokers and moneylenders robbed peasants of the small profits they realized from their crops. Many had to give up their land to repay debts. Adding to the misery, French officials drafted peasants for hard labor on public works such as road building. Landless peasants and poor laborers had few choices. Some fended off starvation by working under appalling conditions on French-owned rubber plantations or in the coal mines of Tonkin.

THESE MEN PACKAGE RUBBER AT A PLANTATION IN VIETNAM IN 1890. MANY PLANTATION OWNERS TREATED THEIR WORKERS HARSHLY.

French colonialism in Vietnam was in some ways less harsh than colonialism in other empires. Those Vietnamese who learned French and accepted French culture became members of an elite, entitled to good jobs and education. Some even became French citizens. The French gave preferential treatment to Vietnam's sizable Catholic minority.

But Vietnamese participation in administering the country and economy was limited. French officials ran Vietnam, backed by French-controlled police and French colonial military forces. French and Chinese business owners and a Vietnamese landowner class dominated the economy.

"Civilizing Duty"

AS THE FRENCH PREMIER during much of the 1880s, Jules Ferry presided over the expansion of the French Empire. In 1884 he defended his nation's colonial efforts this way: "The policy of colonial expansion is a political and economic system . . . connected to . . . economic ideas; the most far-reaching ideas of civilization; and ideas of a political and patriotic sort."

He also expressed an idea that was popular among many westerners of this era—the notion that white Europeans were superior to nonwhites. He believed: "The higher races have a right over the lower races. . . . They have the duty to civilize the inferior races. . . . European nations acquit themselves with generosity, with grandeur, and with sincerity of this superior civilizing duty."

The French Empire

FRANCE'S OVERSEAS EMPIRE IN 1914 was second only to Great Britain's, with roughly sixty million people and 4 million square miles (10.4 million sq. km) of territory. In addition to Indochina, France controlled the North African countries of Tunisia, Algeria, and Morocco, as well as vast territories farther south in Africa. France also held French Guiana in South America and islands in the Pacific Ocean.

THE VIETNAMESE RESISTANCE MOVEMENT

Armed resistance aimed at expelling the French invaders arose at the end of the nineteenth century, but efforts to restore an independent Vietnam were unsuccessful. In the early twentieth century, the resistance movement took heart from developments farther north in Asia. Japan defeated the Russian Empire during a war in 1905, showing that a modernized Asian society could overcome a European power. In China, revolutionaries overthrew the ruling family in 1911 and set up a republic, a nation with a president and elected officials. This event encouraged Vietnamese nationalists—people desiring self-rule for Vietnam. But the French police kept a careful eye on any Vietnamese demanding independence from France, and Vietnamese nationalists largely had to operate underground or abroad.

Also in 1911, a young Vietnamese nationalist left Vietnam, working his way to Europe and the United States as a ship's crewman. Wandering, absorbing foreign cultures, learning languages, and educating himself, the young man used a variety of traditional Vietnamese names, made-up names, and foreign names. He eventually combined a common Vietnamese name (Ho) and the Vietnamese words for "will" and" "enlightenment" to identify himself as Ho Chi Minh. He presented himself as a man of the people, a determined revolutionary, and a person of high ideals and learning.

In 1914 World War I (1914–1918) broke out in Europe. When the war ended, Ho Chi Minh was living in Paris, France, the site of peace talks following the war. The U.S. delegation to the 1919 meeting was headed by President Woodrow Wilson. Wilson favored the principle of self-determination—that is, letting people in each specific territory determine their own political futures.

Ho passed on a request to Wilson, asking simply that the Vietnamese people be granted basic rights and have some say in determining their own affairs. The appeal had no impact, however, as British and French leaders drawing up the peace treaty opposed self-determination for their African and Asian colonies.

In 1920 Ho joined the newly formed French Communist Party. Communism is a political system in which the state controls all business and economic activity and, in theory, distributes a nation's resources equally to all people. Ho was inspired by events in Russia, where revolutionaries led by Vladimir Lenin had set up a Communist government in 1917. The new government, eventually called the Union of Soviet Socialist Republics, or Soviet Union, became the headquarters of the Comintern, an international Communist movement. Its aim was to overthrow capitalism—or private enterprise—worldwide.

Young Communist

Communist beliefs, based on the writings of nineteenth-century German philosopher Karl Marx and Friedrich Engels, held that deepening divisions and contradictions in capitalist, industrial societies would lead to a class struggle—a struggle that the working class would inevitably win. The common people would then establish a Communist state. In this state, the government—which represented all people—would own the means of production: factories, farms, and other sources of wealth.

Marxist theory also described how capitalist societies—such as the great powers of Europe—exploited labor forces, markets, and resources in less-developed nations. As Lenin explained in 1916, "A handful of wealthy countries—England, France, the United States and Germany—have developed monopoly to vast proportions . . . they 'ride on the backs' of hundreds and hundreds of millions of people in other countries and fight among themselves for the division of the . . . spoils." Under Marxist theory, over-throwing foreign domination and opposing worldwide capitalism were linked. This message impressed Ho Chi Minh, who soon became a dedicated Marxist.

Ho spent much of 1924 in Moscow, Russia, the capital of the Soviet Union. There he met Soviet leaders and was welcomed as a fellow Marxist and revolutionary. He continued to absorb Communist theory

Ho Chi Minh, shown here in 1924, went to the Soviet Union to learn more about Communism.

and came to believe that Vietnam was beginning a long struggle, with years of organizing ahead before the "favorable moment" arrived for expelling the French and undertaking a Communist revolution.

Ho's next base was Canton in southern China, where he assisted the Soviet adviser to Chiang Kai-shek, leader of the Chinese nationalists. Chiang was dedicated to modernizing China and freeing it from foreign domination. A non-Communist, he had an uneasy alliance with China's Communists, led by Mao Zedong.

Ho returned to the Soviet Union after Chiang Kai-shek turned on Mao's Communists in 1927, killing thousands. Other Communists escaped and regrouped in safer parts of China. From remote bases, Mao began to train his followers in guerrilla warfare—that is, warfare conducted by small bands of fighters, using tactics such as ambushes, raids, and bombings. Mao also promoted his doctrine of a "people's war," which relied for victory on guerrilla tactics and long-term support of ordinary people.

People's War

CHINESE COMMUNIST LEADER MAO ZEDONG wrote a prescription for a "people's war," which Ho Chi Minh and other Communist leaders would follow. His rules were as follows:

1. Destroy weak and isolated enemy forces first, strong enemy forces later.
2. Control smaller cities and rural areas first, big cities later.
3. Wiping out the enemy's forces is more important than holding or seizing cities.
4. Concentrate an absolutely superior force. Encircle the enemy forces and wipe them out.
5. Fight no battle you are not sure of winning.

MAO ZEDONG IN 1925

CHAPTER 3

Time for Revolution

BY 1930 ECONOMIC CONDITIONS had worsened in Vietnam and the misery of many Vietnamese was deepening. The plight of the peasants was grim. Absentee landlords owned much of the farmland. After paying their rent (either with money or part of their harvest), peasants had barely enough left over for survival, even during years of good harvest. During bad years, famine was never far away and thousands died of starvation. Many people lived in debt, and peasants who could not pay their taxes sometimes went to jail.

French rule was politically oppressive for most Vietnamese. The Vietnamese had no say in government at any level. The authorities could jail them for only suspicion of criminal activity. The authorities also monitored all newspapers and public gatherings to make sure that no one spoke out openly against the government.

Ho returned to southern China to gather Vietnamese Communists into a united movement. The Communists found a receptive audience for their message. They explained that the suffering of landless peasants and exploited workers in Vietnam was due to oppressive French rule. They charged that French colonialists had denied the Vietnamese people independence and individual rights and had reduced them to poverty, while at the same time, the French became wealthy from Vietnamese labor and resources. From the Communist point of view, expelling the French and remedying Vietnam's social ills went hand in hand.

The year 1930 was a pivotal one for the Vietnamese independence movement. In secret meetings in Hong Kong, China, Ho Chi Minh brought together various Communist organizations to create the Vietnamese Communist Party (soon renamed the Indochinese Communist Party). Also in 1930, Vietnamese soldiers under the leadership of the Vietnamese Nationalist Party revolted against French rule. Later in the year, under Communist leadership, desperate peasants revolted against their landlords. The French ruthlessly crushed both risings, but the Communists continued to organize and expand their influence.

Ho Chi Minh was above all a dedicated Communist, but he shared the goals of all Vietnamese nationalists. We can see this mix of goals in his 1932 agenda for the Indochinese Communist Party. The agenda called for:

- Complete independence for all countries of Indochina and withdrawal of French forces
- The end of governance by mandarins, nobles, and ruling families in Vietnam, Cambodia, and Laos
- A government and army made up of workers and peasants

- Nationalization (government takeover) of foreign-owned banks, companies, plantations, and transportation systems
- Confiscation of all lands owned by French businesses, Catholic missions, landowners, moneylenders, royal families, mandarins, and nobles
- Cancellation of workers' debts and government debts
- Self-determination for Cambodians, Laotians, and other Indochinese peoples
- An eight-hour working day; better working conditions; health, old-age, and unemployment insurance; and labor unions
- Complete equality for Indochinese women
- Support for revolutionary movements in China and India

WHIRLWIND OF CHANGE: WORLD WAR II

World War II (1939–1945) began in Europe on September 1, 1939, when Germany invaded Poland. France fell to a German invasion in May 1940. The French government under Premier Philippe Pétain agreed to cooperate with Germany. Under the agreement, a German army occupied much of France, and Pétain ran the French government from the city of Vichy in central France. A rival Free French movement, claiming to be the legitimate government of France in exile, sprang up in Great Britain under General Charles de Gaulle.

Throughout the war, France retained its colonial empire and the military forces stationed there. In Vietnam and other French possessions, French officials obeyed the Vichy government. The Vichy regime appointed Admiral Jean Decoux governor of Indochina in July 1940.

Japan, a German ally, had been fighting to conquer China since 1937. The Japanese wanted to use Vietnam to support their campaigns in China and wanted to block the shipment of war goods through Vietnam to China. The Japanese demanded that Decoux cooperate with them, and because France had been conquered by Germany and was weak in Indochina, he had to accept. At first, the Japanese stationed troops and used air bases in northern Vietnam but let the French maintain their government and military forces there. In 1941 the Japanese extended their occupation into the rest of the country.

As the war raged around them, Ho Chi Minh and his fellow Vietnamese Communists organized a coalition of anticolonialist movements in May 1941. The new organization was called Viet Nam

JAPANESE TROOPS ENTER THE CITY OF SAIGON ON BICYCLES IN 1941. DURING WORLD WAR II, JAPAN OCCUPIED VIETNAM.

Doc Lap Dong Minh Hoi, shortened to Viet Minh. The Vietnamese Communists dominated the movement and provided the core leadership, and gradually the name Viet Minh came to stand for the Vietnamese Communists and other Communist forces fighting the French in Vietnam.

SHIFTING SANDS

In mid-1941, Japan used Vietnam as a springboard for its campaigns in Southeast Asia. Japan demanded more access to Vietnam's rice, rubber, and other resources. The French again had little choice but to cooperate. Japan widened the war in December 1941 by attacking U.S., British, and Dutch territories in Asia and the Pacific.

All the while, Ho Chi Minh continued to organize. In 1942 he went to China to get help from Chiang Kai-shek's Nationalist government, then in an uncomfortable wartime alliance with Mao Zedong's Communists against the Japanese. A suspicious-looking foreigner, Ho was arrested and passed on to a Nationalist general, who jailed him for being a Communist agitator. But impressed with Ho's abilities and sincerity, the general soon asked him to form a broad anti-Japanese movement, including both the Viet Minh and non-Communist Vietnamese independence groups.

By the beginning of 1945, Germany and Japan were clearly approaching defeat. In March, as Japan's military position worsened, the Japanese worried that the French in Vietnam might attack them. Ending their policy of coexistence, the Japanese turned on French forces and administrators in Vietnam. They disarmed and imprisoned French troops, killing those who resisted. Japanese authorities then had the figurehead Vietnamese emperor, Bao Dai of the Nguyen dynasty, declare Vietnam's independence and form a puppet government under Japanese control.

A Favorable Moment

Germany surrendered to the Allies in May 1945. Flush with their victory in Europe, Allied leaders of the three great powers—Great Britain, the United States, and the Soviet Union—met in Potsdam, Germany, in July. As part of many decisions on the fate of postwar Asia, they agreed to move Allied forces into Vietnam to disarm Japanese soldiers and return them to Japan.

By this time, Ho was back in Vietnam, hiding out in the mountain jungles of northern Tonkin. In the final months of the war, he and the Viet Minh assisted the Allies by reporting on Japanese movements and helping downed Allied pilots. The United States encouraged the Viet Minh's anti-Japanese activities. It sent a group of U.S. military specialists, called the Deer Team, to consult with the Viet Minh and to train the Vietnamese in guerrilla operations.

Ho sensed a "favorable moment" for revolutionary action when the Japanese surrendered to the Allies in August 1945. With the French military neutralized in Vietnam (and many French troops still

No Deal

IN HIS YOUTH, Ho Chi Minh lived in Brooklyn, New York; and London, England. He spoke English and several other languages well. Upset that the Americans had slipped in a French agent among the Deer Team members, Ho complained in English, "Look, who are you guys trying to kid? This guy's not part of the deal."

imprisoned) and Japanese forces surrendering, there was little to stop a Viet Minh takeover.

Blocking efforts by elements of Bao Dai's government to take control, on September 2, before cheering crowds in Hanoi, Ho Chi Minh proclaimed the establishment of the Democratic Republic of Vietnam. Vietnam's last emperor, Bao Dai, gave up his throne to become an ordinary citizen.

Vietnam, it seemed, was free. The Viet Minh hurriedly organized military units and took over key areas while they set up the apparatus of government. Japanese soldiers still stationed in Vietnam did little to hinder the Viet Minh takeover. They sometimes even helped the Viet Minh by turning over important buildings and facilities as well as weapons. At least in the North, Vietnam was falling into the hands of the Viet Minh. The situation in the South was more complicated.

The French Return

Saigon in southern Vietnam had been France's first point of entry into Vietnam and was a center of French economic interests. The city was home to many French and other Europeans. When the Viet Minh tried to assert their authority in Saigon as the rightful leaders of Vietnam, many French people there reacted with disgust.

What's more, the restored French government, headed by Charles de Gaulle after World War II, intended to reestablish France to the status of a great power. That meant reasserting control of the French Empire, including Vietnam. The British, with troublesome independence movements in their own colonies, were sympathetic to France's colonial ambitions. The United States took more of a hands-off approach. It viewed Indochina as a French problem and took little interest in

Change of Policy

FRANKLIN D. ROOSEVELT, U.S. president through most of World War II, had opposed having the United States help restore or maintain European colonial empires. He signed on to the 1941 Atlantic Charter, which recognized the right of all people to self-determination, or self-government. "The case of Indo-China is perfectly clear," he said in 1944. "France has milked it for one hundred years. The people of Indo-China are entitled to something better than that."

Roosevelt died in April 1945. The new U.S. president, Harry S. Truman, was less concerned than Roosevelt with dismantling colonial empires. Under Truman the United States supported colonial independence in principle while avoiding actions that might upset its allies.

France's return to Vietnam. More important for the United States was restoring France as a power that could help stabilize postwar Europe.

Soon after the Japanese surrender, British forces arrived in Saigon to disarm Japanese troops there, and French troops were not far behind. Tensions quickly grew between the French and the Viet Minh. As the friction grew, British general Douglas Gracey agreed to French requests for help in restoring order—and French rule—in Vietnam.

The British cracked down on Vietnamese political activity and shut down newspapers. Gracey also freed French troops who had been imprisoned by the Japanese. Rearmed after suffering months of captivity, the French soldiers were looking for trouble. French civilians were also infuriated by Viet Minh claims to authority and their threats to French interests. Some French civilians joined the soldiers to seize key buildings from the Viet Minh and randomly attack Vietnamese.

The Viet Minh responded with a military strike that shut down Saigon. Tens of thousands of French residents cowered as the Viet Minh attacked French facilities across the city. The Viet Minh even helped a group of gangsters called the Binh Xuyen enter a guarded French neighborhood and kill or kidnap hundreds of French civilians.

The violence made France's government even more determined to reimpose French authority. De Gaulle appointed Admiral Georges Thierry d'Argenlieu to head the civil administration in Vietnam and put World War II hero General Philippe Leclerc in charge of French forces. Leclerc moved quickly to shatter Viet Minh control of the South.

The Viet Minh withdrew, but they also used terror to remind villagers who really controlled Vietnam. Viet Minh guerrillas attacked French posts, reasserting control wherever the French were weak. The French soon restored their government, however. At the same time, d'Argenlieu brought some Vietnamese into the administration.

Ho Hangs On

In the North, the Viet Minh survived and kept their forces in place. But Ho Chi Minh faced a terrible dilemma. With little support for Vietnamese independence from the Western powers and with the French massing military forces to restore French rule in the North, he had to make a deal with France.

In a March 1946 treaty, Ho agreed to less than the full independence from France that he had been fighting for. Instead, Vietnam would become a "free" member of an Indochinese Federation within the French Union (the old French Empire). In name, Vietnam would be an independent state, but in reality, it would still be controlled by

France. Ho also agreed to allow substantial French forces to remain in Vietnam for five years.

Ho had cut a bitter deal, but the French were not finished. They told Ho to bring a delegation to Paris to negotiate the unresolved issues of Vietnam's independence. Yet another betrayal was in the works.

HO CHI MINH MADE A DEAL FOR LESS THAN FULL INDEPENDENCE FROM FRANCE IN 1946.

CHAPTER 4

A New War

A S FRENCH FORCES BUILT UP in Vietnam, the French leadership there—and increasingly in Paris—wanted to limit Vietnamese independence and keep as much control of the nation as possible. In June 1946, d'Argenlieu created a separate Republic of Cochin China in southern Vietnam. Supposedly independent, the republic was actually controlled by the French and was largely a device to protect French interests. Soon after, he held the conference in Paris with handpicked representatives from the countries of Indochina, including Ho Chi Minh.

The meeting in Paris yielded little, and after two months, most of the Viet Minh delegation left for home. Staying behind for one last effort, Ho felt he had no choice but to sign the Fontainebleau Agreement on September 19, 1946. The agreement guaranteed French economic and civil advantages in Vietnam, maintained the privileged position of French language and culture, and required the Vietnamese to take part in a French-controlled Indochinese Union in which Vietnamese independence was still limited. The newly created Republic of Cochin China, being solidly in the French sphere of influence, was not included in the agreement. Feeling the Viet Minh had no choice, Ho accepted the agreement and left France disheartened.

COUNTDOWN TO WAR

When French forces arrived in northern Vietnam as part of the March 1946 agreement, they found themselves facing off against Viet Minh units there. The tense situation exploded when Vietnamese and French forces clashed in the port of Haiphong over the question of who could enforce customs laws. The incident escalated as the French tried to seize all of Haiphong. After a cease-fire, d'Argenlieu flew to Paris and got the French government to authorize strong military action.

On November 23, the local French commander told the Viet Minh to pull out of Haiphong or be crushed. French warships then shelled Haiphong while French aircraft cleared out resistance to tank-supported French infantry. After four days of heavy combat, Haiphong was in French hands and thousands of Vietnamese were dead.

While the local French command made plans to seize Hanoi, Ho Chi Minh appealed to French prime minister Léon Blum to stop the fighting, but French officials in Vietnam blocked the message. A Viet Minh attack on French civilians and facilities on December 19 brought a massive French response, and bitter fighting for Hanoi went on for weeks. The Viet Minh commander, Vo Nguyen Giap—a former teacher with no military background—sent in units to battle the French, while the French poured in troops, aircraft, and supplies.

Soon the French held the populated region of the Red River delta in the North. Viet Minh units retired to rugged areas along the Chinese border and the mountain jungles in the northwestern part of Tonkin—the Viet Bac. In hiding, Ho called on Viet Minh forces to resist as he also tried to get French politicians and France's allies to end the fighting.

VIET MINH COMMANDER VO NGUYEN GIAP LED TROOPS AGAINST THE FRENCH IN THE INDOCHINA WAR.

THE FIRST PHASE

The Indochina War (1946–1954) between France and the Viet Minh had officially begun. The arena of their struggle was Tonkin, or northern Vietnam. The key objectives were control of the Red River floodplain and the uplands and valleys where the Viet Minh could hide, emerging to attack the delta when the time was right. The densely populated delta was the traditional heartland of Vietnam. The surrounding hills and mountains, covered with thick jungle, were nearly impenetrable for regular French units with their heavy vehicles. The rugged uplands bordered Laos to the west. To the north lay China, where by then Chiang Kai-shek's Nationalists and Mao Zedong's Communists were locked in a civil war.

At first, French successes in chasing the Viet Minh from the Red River delta area and their continued military buildup seemed to be paying off. The French held their own militarily and at times went on the offensive. A 1947 French campaign, which included the use of airborne forces coordinated with French advances up river valleys, nearly overran the Communists' Viet Bac sanctuary in northwestern Tonkin. Viet Minh units based in the refuge managed to slip away from French forces trying to block and engage them. The French nearly captured top Viet Minh leaders, including Ho Chi Minh.

French military planners soon realized that they lacked the personnel and resources to find and destroy Viet Minh forces in their

THIS FRENCH SHIP BROUGHT TROOPS TO VIETNAM IN 1947, AS TENSIONS ESCALATED BETWEEN THE FRENCH AND THE VIET MINH.

remote hiding places. Entering the Viet Bac or similar areas was risky for French forces. The Viet Minh could already draw on more troop strength than the French. As they gained experience using larger units, the Viet Minh learned that with careful planning and rapid movement, they could concentrate a larger force than the French had at any given point and overwhelm the enemy. In keeping with Mao's doctrine of the "people's war," the Viet Minh could also disperse into the jungle if the battle turned against them.

While the Viet Minh organized militarily, they also worked politically. They pursued a patient strategy of building up their grassroots organization, including teaching villagers about Communist doctrine.

Halfway around the world in France, the often changing and weak French governments contributed to uncertainty over foreign policy. The war in Indochina was becoming unpopular in France, and public support declined steadily as the fighting continued. French Communists and others who opposed colonialism in particular began to speak out against the war. Money was also a major problem. French forces in Indochina used up much of France's annual military budget—money desperately needed for French forces in Europe.

Getting enough troops to Vietnam was also a problem. French policies limited the overseas use of French draftees performing their required military service, so French forces in Indochina were made up of volunteers. These were a mix of French enlisted and career soldiers, non-French personnel serving in units of the legendary Foreign Legion, and units recruited in French territories in Africa. Recruiting Vietnamese for service in the French military eased the shortfall in troops, but the French never had the hundreds of thousands of reliable troops that they needed to both protect the countryside and go after and destroy the Viet Minh.

Élysée and Afterward

In March 1949, France moved forward with a new plan for a unified Vietnamese government. With the Élysée Agreement, France formed the Associated State of Vietnam, joining Cochin China, Annam, and Tonkin, with the former emperor Bao Dai at its head. The French hoped the new arrangement would satisfy Vietnamese hopes for a unified and independent country and would lure support from the Viet Minh. The French still wanted to control the new state to the advantage of France and French colonial interests in Vietnam, however, and the agreement left France in charge of important government

FORMER VIETNAMESE EMPEROR BAO DAI WAS NAMED HEAD OF THE ASSOCIATED STATE OF VIETNAM IN 1949.

functions. Vietnam was to be an independent state but in name only.

The political maneuvers did not satisfy the Viet Minh, who were determined to win complete independence for Vietnam. In the North, the fighting continued. The French built up their forces, secured their hold on the Red River delta, and constructed a network of fortified posts. In the delta, the French could reinforce these posts quickly, bringing in armored vehicles along a network of roads. In remote valleys, however, fortified posts were hard to reinforce quickly—and were tempting targets for attacks by massed Viet Minh forces.

The Viet Minh continued building up their strength and their connections throughout Vietnamese society. They developed an intelligence network using thousands of local informants, some employed by the French. As recruits swelled their ranks, the Viet Minh created main-force units that could go toe-to-toe with the French army. The Viet Minh also organized local and regional forces that could support their main campaigns and harass the French at every turn. At every level, political officers (or commissars, a Soviet term) explained the Viet Minh cause, watched for signs of disloyalty, and encouraged the revolutionary spirit of villagers and Viet Minh units alike.

The Viet Minh developed an impressive network of supply systems, arm depots, and weapons factories, as well as an effective communications network. In secure areas, Viet Minh engineers improved vital supply routes. All the while, the Viet Minh probed and tested French forces as they built up larger units and gained experience. By 1949 the Viet Minh were strong enough to defend their Viet Bac refuge while forging a national army that could directly challenge the French. Soon it would be time to strike.

The Chinese Connection

Victorious after a three-year civil war, the Chinese Communist Party, led by Mao Zedong, proclaimed the establishment of the People's Republic of China in October 1949. The victory left Chinese Communist armies on the northern border of Vietnam.

Militarily, the French found their situation completely changed. The Chinese could send aid to their fellow Communists, the Viet Minh, through the rugged country along Vietnam's border—an area impossible for the French to control. Previously, the Viet Minh had depended on a trickle of outside supplies, captured French weapons, and locally acquired food. But with Chinese support, they could get Chinese-supplied arms, uniforms, and provisions to equip larger and larger units.

Chinese material support made the Viet Minh a force to be reckoned with. In 1950 Ho Chi Minh and Vo Nguyen Giap visited China, which had just recognized the Viet Minh as the legitimate government of Vietnam. (The Soviet Union also recognized Ho's government that year.) The Chinese agreed to provide more war materials, training, and advisers. They shipped weapons and munitions along improved roads and railroads near the border.

Another benefit was that thousands of Viet Minh soldiers could be trained in China, safe from French attack. In addition, Chinese advisers placed with Viet Minh units gave guidance on tactics while technical specialists helped the Viet Minh operate new equipment.

The Cold War Heats Up

By this time, the United States had grown fearful of the spread of Communism around the world. On the Korea Peninsula in Asia, which had been split into North and South Korea following World War II, Soviet-backed Communist forces from the North invaded the South in June 1950. The North Koreans planned to seize South Korea and unify the entire peninsula under a Communist regime.

The North Korean attack was halted when U.S. president Harry Truman committed U.S. forces and asked the United Nations (UN) to defend South Korea. When a successful UN offensive forced retreating North Korean armies nearly to the border with China, Mao Zedong ordered hundreds of thousands of Chinese "volunteer" troops to assist the North Korean Communists. The conflict would rage in Korea for two more years, and the battlefields of that war became another source of supply for the Viet Minh, with captured U.S. vehicles and weapons being funneled through China to Vietnam.

U.S. TROOPS CROSS SNOWY MOUNTAINS IN SOUTH KOREA IN 1951. THE UNITED STATES, ALONG WITH UN FORCES, FOUGHT COMMUNISTS ON THE KOREA PENINSULA FOR THREE YEARS.

The battle between Communist and non-Communist governments—led by the Soviet Union and the United States, respectively—was called the Cold War (1945–1991). With the backing of both China and the Soviet Union, and with their Communist doctrine, the Viet Minh clearly sided with the Communist forces in that war.

The United States had been frustrated with France's refusal to give Vietnam genuine independence, but the new links with China and the Soviet Union made U.S. leaders take a stronger stance against the Viet Minh. The United States viewed the Viet Minh's fight for Vietnamese independence as part of the larger Cold War struggle, and when Communist governments recognized Ho's Democratic Republic of Vietnam, the United States was alarmed. Chinese aid to the Viet Minh, the possibility of China intervening militarily in Vietnam, and the mixed performance of French forces there also alarmed U.S. leaders.

In response to Soviet and Chinese recognition of Ho's government, the United States recognized Bao Dai's national government—the Associated State of Vietnam. The United States sent diplomatic representatives to the new country, even though it was obviously controlled by France. Some U.S. diplomats doubted the new government's prospects for survival, but the threat of Communism advancing from China helped convince the United States to take sides.

As the tempo of combat with the Viet Minh accelerated and the costs of fighting soared, the French pleaded with the United States for money and military help. U.S. leaders overcame their distaste for colonialism and came to accept the French position that they were helping an independent Vietnamese government resist a Communist takeover. Substantial U.S. aid—some for Bao Dai's new government but much of it for the French military effort—was soon on the way to Vietnam. (Bao Dai pocketed some U.S. aid money for his personal use.)

Chinese support, the start of the Korean War (1950–1953), and the widening Cold War had changed the nature of the conflict in Vietnam. Viet Minh forces trained safely inside China, and Chinese-supplied weapons, ammunition, and other materials enabled the Viet Minh to field an army of roughly one hundred thousand full-time soldiers, supported by regional and local forces.

Beginning with a single regiment in 1947, by 1950 Giap had organized the People's Army of Vietnam (PAVN) into several divisions of around ten thousand men each. The PAVN was very much a light infantry army, but as supplies improved, troops had access to more machine guns and mortars. The PAVN formed specialized artillery units that added enormously to its offensive punch.

Logistics and engineering support were basic but met the PAVN's needs. Engineering units built and maintained supply routes as well as tunnels and camps in base areas. For transportation, the PAVN moved mainly on foot, although the Chinese and Soviets began to provide some trucks. Without much motorized transport, PAVN troops were not tied to the roads as the French were and could move across the rugged countryside, hiding from French air attacks and disappearing into the jungle after surprising French columns.

A vast army of porters—tens of thousands of men and women—sustained the Viet Minh campaigns. These laborers carried supplies on their backs or pushed heavily loaded bicycles along the Viet Minh's network of supply trails and dirt roads.

Political officers traveled with every unit. They observed and reported on the loyalty of soldiers and officers while at the same time providing political education and morale building for the troops.

Battle for the Roads

Starting from nothing, the Viet Minh had built a true people's army. It was, at last, time to use it. In 1950 bitter fighting along French-built roads (*routes coloniales,* or RCs) through rugged northern Tonkin showed that the Viet Minh were no longer a ragtag guerrilla band but a genuine national army.

With their base areas secure, the Viet Minh began launching major offensives. With large and well-supplied forces at his disposal, Giap knew he had to freely sacrifice the lives of his soldiers to inflict heavy losses on the French. He believed that when French losses in troops and money became unbearable, they would leave.

The Viet Minh may not have been ready to launch a decisive general offensive on the Red River plains and seize Hanoi, but they showed themselves masters at achieving local superiority. In attacks on isolated posts and convoys, the Viet Minh used careful planning and superior numbers to overwhelm French troops. French forces—some of them elite Foreign Legion units—defended themselves in fierce fighting. Positions sometimes changed hands several times a day. The scale and tempo of combat were clearly increasing.

Giap focused on French positions in the north of Tonkin. The French had fortified a series of posts running northwest in the Cao Bang region along the Chinese border, from Lang Son to That Khe to Dong Khe and finally to the village of Cao Bang. Viet Minh attacks against these posts cost the Communists heavy losses. But the French found that preserving the posts stretched their resources too thin. The French realized that, with their limited resources and troop strength, they could never control the border, so the posts were of little military value. The French abandoned minor posts and consolidated forces

Homeschooling

VO NGUYEN GIAP is considered one of the most brilliant military commanders of modern times. Yet he acquired most of his skills from reading military classics rather than from formal schooling. He claimed, "I was a self-taught general."

into larger positions. They then decided to vacate the entire area and pull back their troops along RC4, the route that linked their isolated strongpoints.

Alerted to French preparations, Giap struck first. Repeating his success in taking and briefly holding a French fort at Dong Khe earlier that year, Giap sent in massed attacks that overwhelmed the fort's Foreign Legion defenders. A French relief column in Lang Son moved to retake Dong Khe, while French forces in the farthest outpost, Cao Bang, moved southeast along RC4 to join the relief column at Dong Khe.

The retiring French force from Cao Bang, slowed down by terrified civilians and cumbersome vehicles, struggled southeast along the narrow dirt road in a fighting retreat. The Viet Minh concentrated their forces at choke points in a series of large-scale ambushes. French forces counterattacked fiercely to relieve units under assault and to take high ground protecting the column, but the Viet Minh's numbers and ferocity in pressing home attacks at any cost seemed to make them unstoppable.

A massive Viet Minh infantry force halted the relief column from Lang Son. In an ominous sign, the Viet Minh used artillery that they had dragged, pulled, and carried in unseen by the French. The French worked their way around Giap's blocking force and linked up with the Cao Bang column, but the fight along RC4 turned into a massacre as the Viet Minh overwhelmed unit after unit. Crack French infantry and paratroop battalions were nearly wiped out, reduced to a few survivors who escaped through the jungle. With more than five thousand killed or missing, thousands more wounded, and the loss of countless weapons, the expedition was a French military catastrophe—and a signal that the war was entering a new phase.

CHAPTER 5

Prelude to Dien Bien Phu

THE DISASTER ALONG RC4 forced the French government to react strongly. It gave complete military and civil authority to one of France's most experienced generals, Jean de Lattre de Tassigny. De Lattre brought an overall strategy and aggressiveness that had been previously lacking. The morale of French forces began to improve.

De Lattre also brought luck—and a talent for exploiting the mistakes of his opponent. An overly optimistic Giap decided to follow up on his successes on RC4 with a bold move into the Red River delta early in 1951. Approaching through the mountains and hills to within 30 miles (48 km) of Hanoi, two Viet Minh divisions seized strongpoints around the town of Vinh Yen—territory the Communists needed to control if they wanted to continue a drive on Hanoi, push out the French, and end the war.

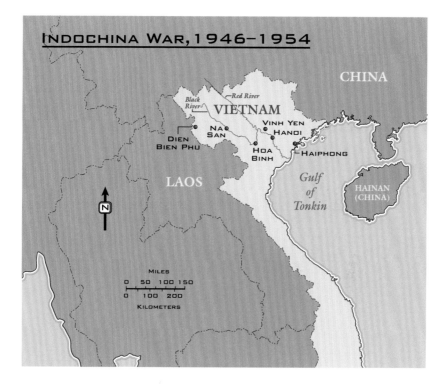

Indochina War, 1946–1954

Giap's divisions tried to overwhelm French positions in terrifying "human wave" assaults. In these assaults, thousands of Viet Minh attackers rushed toward the French, hoping to swamp them with sheer numbers, but the French stopped them with air strikes and an equally terrifying new weapon—napalm bombs. These fiery bombs contained jellied fuel. When they burst among the Viet Minh attackers, thousands were burned alive. Survivors were shocked and demoralized. The attacks stalled, and Viet Minh units faded back into the hills.

Giap had to admit defeat at Vinh Yen. His losses did not stop him, however. The Viet Minh were by then in a neck-and-neck race with the French. As the Viet Minh received Chinese-supplied weapons and training, the French kept pace by procuring U.S. equipment and money.

Liquid Fire

THE ALLIES FIRST USED napalm bombs near the end of World War II. Made by mixing gasoline or other fuels with a gelling agent, napalm bombs proved to be a devastating way to stop human wave attacks in Vietnam and Korea. After the bombs exploded, the jellied gasoline flowed into trenches and stuck to victims' skin. Some of the most famous and horrifying photographs of the Vietnam War (1957–1975) show soldiers and civilians burned by napalm. For French ground forces in the Indochina War, napalm often spelled the difference between survival and destruction.

NAPALM BOMBS BURST OVER TRENCHES OCCUPIED BY VIET MINH AT DIEN BIEN PHU IN 1954.

With his new divisions, Giap was willing to gamble and trade heavy losses for a chance to eject the French.

The Viet Minh launched an offensive toward Haiphong. But bombardments from French naval vessels offshore and French forces' stubborn defense of a fortified village slowed the advance. With hundreds of Viet Minh attackers dead, Giap abandoned the costly offensive.

Next, Giap lunged for the delta area along the Day River in the delta's southeastern corner. His goal was to smash thinly held French positions in the area and assert Viet Minh control. Giap was able to employ three divisions as well as two independent regiments for the operation. At some French positions, the Viet Minh surprised and overwhelmed the defenders. Others held their ground at the cost of many French dead, including de Lattre's son. The Viet Minh also attacked vessels that the French brought up the Day River. After suffering heavy losses, the Viet Minh again retired to the safety of the hills.

Once again, a quick and forceful French response under de Lattre had prevented the annihilation of French units and denied territory to the Viet Minh. De Lattre had used French firepower and mobility to beat the Viet Minh at their own game—catching the enemy in "meat grinder" battles that inflicted a terrible cost in fighting units shattered and human lives destroyed.

De Lattre was too seasoned a commander to relax the pressure and let the Viet Minh recover. He knew he had to bring Giap to battle again. Moving quickly to catch the Viet Minh off balance, in November 1951, he dropped three parachute battalions on the town of Hoa Binh and sent a major infantry force, supported by two units of river vessels, up the Black River valley to join them. Hoa Binh was a local center for the pro-French Muong ethnic group. The region was remote. The only access was up the narrow Black River valley

France's Inland Navy

THE FRENCH USED CONVERTED World War II landing craft and small boats, armored and armed with a variety of weapons, to carry troops and equipment up Vietnam's many small rivers. These "Dinassaut" units (short for Division Navale d'Assaut, or Division of Naval Assault) played a useful role in several French campaigns. Later, U.S. forces in Vietnam tried the same approach, patrolling the Mekong Delta with swift boats and other navy vessels. (U.S. senator and presidential candidate John Kerry commanded a swift boat when he served in Vietnam.)

or across a range of rugged mountains.

The French had earlier abandoned Hoa Binh to the Viet Minh. This time Giap chose not to defend the area, and the French retook the town against light opposition.

FORCING BATTLE, INFLICTING PAIN

French military planners desperately needed a victory if France were to retain a presence in Vietnam on French terms. A large percentage of France's military budget was being poured into Vietnam. Military leaders had to convince the French National Assembly that a military solution was possible—and worth continued funding. A French victory was also important to impress the U.S. Congress, whose members were debating whether to greatly expand U.S. funding and military aid for the French effort in Vietnam.

Giap also understood these issues. He knew he had to keep raising the cost of the Indochina War until it was unbearable for France. He believed that after much wasted money, many deaths, and much frustration, the French would give up hopes for a military solution and leave Vietnam.

At Hoa Binh, Giap saw an opportunity to ratchet up the pressure on France. He acted quickly. In an impressive feat of movement, logistics, and concealment, three Viet Minh divisions converged on Hoa Binh. Two more moved in from the northwest and southeast. Along with local, part-time units, they harassed and blocked French lines of communication. Giap had in place a superior force with which to inflict serious losses on the French.

Viet Minh human wave assaults overran a French outpost in the Black River valley, killing many defenders and leaving hundreds of attackers dead. Powerful French sweeps (large-scale patrols) sent to

FRENCH TROOPS COME ASHORE IN RAFTS AFTER CROSSING THE BLACK RIVER IN 1952. FRENCH TROOPS USED MANY DIFFERENT SEA VESSELS TO NAVIGATE VIETNAM'S RIVERS.

find the Viet Minh met no resistance, however. The Viet Minh simply melted back into the rugged countryside, only to reappear in pinprick attacks on isolated posts. After the French abandoned one bank of the Black River, the Viet Minh poured down a murderous fire on river convoys to Hoa Binh. After that, the French would have to supply Hoa Binh by air—or over the mountains via RC6. Another nightmare road battle was shaping up.

In a carefully planned attack, the Viet Minh swarmed the defenses of a Foreign Legion position on RC6. In fierce fighting, some of it hand to hand, the Legionnaires mowed down hundreds of attackers.

FRENCH GENERAL RAOUL SALAN (LEFT) STANDS WITH BAO DAI DURING A MILITARY CEREMONY IN HANOI IN 1951.

Despite this French success, the Viet Minh could still block the road with large forces and ambush French resupply efforts. A French taskforce sent to clear the route was barely able to fight its way through.

The French command, with General Raoul Salan replacing the mortally ill de Lattre, decided to evacuate Hoa Binh. French losses had far overshadowed the benefits of holding the city. French forces conducted one fighting retreat along RC6 and another with river craft and infantry along the Black River valley, again with substantial losses.

FRENCH FAILURES

The French seizure of Hoa Binh had turned into another fighting retreat with heavy losses. Even inflicting massive Viet Minh casualties had failed to cripple Viet Minh offensive power. The fighting had ground up French units, exhausted the French army, and showed French mobile forces to be road bound and vulnerable. The Viet Minh seemed stronger than ever.

French operations had to quickly shift to a new area. The Viet Minh once again displayed their skill in moving, concealing, and concentrating their forces. This time, they struck in the jungle-covered hills and mountains west of the Red River delta—a land sparsely inhabited by the ethnic Tai minority.

Moving the bulk of three divisions into position, unseen by patrolling French aircraft, Giap launched an attack on the French-held town of Nghia Lo. Taken completely by surprise, the defenders were overwhelmed and had to surrender. The French began evacuating their posts in the area. To slow down the Viet Minh offensive, the French dropped a parachute battalion in the path of the Viet Minh advance. The battalion and a locally recruited unit fought desperate rearguard actions and bought vital time for French forces withdrawing from the area.

The Viet Minh quickly overran the entire region except for a few French strongholds. The French airlifted substantial forces into one of these outposts, Na San, which had an airstrip. In a broad valley near the border with Laos, the Viet Minh seized a minor French post named Dien Bien Phu.

To throw the Viet Minh off balance, the French high command launched Operation Lorraine, an attack toward the northwest, deep into Viet Minh territory. The goal was to threaten the Viet Minh's rear bases and draw in major Viet Minh units to defend them—giving French firepower an opportunity to chew up more Viet Minh units and delay the inevitable Viet Minh offensive toward the Red River delta.

Moving up the Red and then the Clear River valley, French columns supported by armor and river vessels met with airborne units dropped earlier. The combined force pushed on northwest, still unopposed.

While the expedition was successful in overrunning some Viet Minh arms depots, it failed to draw off substantial Viet Minh forces from their invasion of the northwestern highlands. The Viet Minh

FRENCH GENERAL HENRI NAVARRE LAUNCHED OPERATION LORRAINE IN VIETNAM IN 1952. NAVARRE IS SHOWN HERE IN 1953, WHEN HE WAS MADE COMMANDER-IN-CHIEF OF THE FRENCH FORCES IN INDOCHINA.

continued their thrust into the northwestern hill country, reaching the Black River. But aside from some sniping as the French entered the area, the Viet Minh declined to attack in large formations, denying the French a chance for a "meat grinder" battle.

General Salan ordered the columns to retire back down the valley to the safety of the delta. The French troops did not relax, however. They knew from experience that withdrawing through Viet Minh–controlled territory meant a fighting retreat that at any moment could turn into a bloodbath.

As usual, the Viet Minh planned carefully. At a spot where RC2 passed through a narrow valley, the Viet Minh laid a deadly ambush. After paralyzing French armored vehicles with a mortar and artillery barrage, the Viet Minh attacked the center of the strung-out French column. The column's commander ordered infantry attacks to clear the Viet Minh from the high ground. Carried out with bayonet charges, the attacks eventually drove off the Viet Minh. The fighting retreat continued almost to the banks of the Red River. When French forces reentered the delta area, Operation Lorraine came to an end. It would be the largest and last major French ground offensive in Vietnam.

CHAPTER 6

In Search of Battle

THE FRENCH HAD MOVED MAJOR FORCES deep into enemy territory. When forced to retreat, they had narrowly avoided being trapped and annihilated by the Viet Minh. Although the campaign was one more failure to destroy Viet Minh fighting power, the French command would not give up on the idea of annihilating the Viet Minh. They sought a decisive battle that would end the war on French terms.

The officers who planned French strategy were experienced military professionals. They knew their enemy's capabilities and skills were growing, and they knew what that meant in terms of strategy and politics. By this time, the Chinese were trucking tons of supplies to the Viet Minh along roads snaking through rugged Viet Minh–held territory. Porter units moved weapons, ammunition, and supplies where they were needed along a network of trails.

VIETNAMESE PORTERS CARRY FOOD AND MUNITIONS ON BICYCLES TO
VIET MINH TROOPS IN 1954.

The Viet Minh had also made big improvements in firepower.
In addition to captured U.S. artillery from Korea, some Viet Minh
units had automatic weapons, mortars, and recoilless rifles, making
them better equipped than some French infantry units of comparable
size. Light antiaircraft guns of Soviet origin also began to appear on
the battlefields, blunting crucial French advantages in airpower and
air supply.

Time was working against the French in Vietnam both militarily
and politically. Support for the war was dropping steadily in France.
French political leaders knew that it was just a matter of time before

they had to hand over real power to the Vietnamese. However, they thought they could achieve "an honorable exit." They believed they could keep the Viet Minh from becoming the dominant political force in Vietnam and Indochina by breaking Viet Minh military power in one great battle—a final battle.

Na San: Misleading Victory

As a Viet Minh tide swept over the northwestern highlands in late 1952, the small French garrisons in the area fell back on the isolated valley post of Na San. General Salan, the new commander of French forces, decided to turn Na San into a heavily fortified camp that could be supplied by air if Giap's forces cut off road access. Offering Na San as bait for Giap's divisions, Salan built up the valley's defenses to the point where they could maul any attacker. He established a series of strongpoints around a central camp that protected it like the spines of a hedgehog. The French also established positions on the heights surrounding the valley. French engineers improved Na San's small airfield, enabling it to handle cargo aircraft bringing in supplies, troops, and artillery.

Giap took the bait. Two Viet Minh divisions smashed into Na San's defenses and met devastating fire from the French defenders. Decimated by French artillery and air strikes, the attackers withdrew, suffering five hundred dead and thousands wounded.

Na San seemed to show that the "hedgehog" concept worked. French firepower, supplied by air, could destroy Viet Minh forces in the remote backcountry.

More proof of the value of air assault came when a French air-borne force seized Lang Son in May 1953, catching the Viet Minh by

At a cave near Lang Son, French troops discovered a store of Viet Minh arms and ammunition in 1953.

surprise. At Lang Son—abandoned after the disastrous retreat along RC4 in 1950—the French destroyed tons of Viet Minh arms, ammunition, and supplies brought in from nearby China.

At this stage of the war, General Navarre needed victories to back what had by then become the goal of French political leaders—France's retreat from Vietnam on honorable terms. The tools of airborne assault and the air-supported "hedgehog" were some of the few promising options Navarre had left. When Navarre looked for a new place to apply them, he turned to Dien Bien Phu.

Navarre's Plan

The other two parts of Indochina—the kingdoms of Laos and Cambodia—had been quiet for most of the Indochina War. These states were nominally independent but still under heavy French control. In Laos a Communist-dominated independence movement, the Pathet Lao, formed to fight both the French and the Laotian king. In the spring of 1953, Giap sent Viet Minh forces deep into northern Laos to support the Pathet Lao.

The French high command hastily shifted forces to help the Laotians, but it had few airborne units to spare, and the Viet Minh overran some posts in Laos. To block future Viet Minh movements into Laos, General Navarre wanted to establish a strong position on the Vietnam–Laos border. The valley around Dien Bien Phu—a village occupied by the Tai ethnic group—seemed well located for such a role. Mobile French troops could use the fortified camp as a base from which to attack the Viet Minh when they threatened Laos.

Navarre made his decision. In a major airborne assault, Operation Castor, paratroopers of France's most seasoned colonial and Foreign Legion units would land in the valley. Viet Minh units were known to be in the area, and some resistance was possible.

Navarre's plan was to seize an old Japanese-built airstrip in the valley and then quickly drop in combat engineers, equipment, and supplies needed to improve it. An "air bridge" of cargo aircraft could then fly in a stream of troops, materials, and equipment. The base would be able to defend itself against a major assault and also inflict heavy losses on the Viet Minh, allowing the French to negotiate from a position of strength.

Some of Navarre's senior officers had doubts about Operation

Choppers

RECENTLY INTRODUCED IN MILITARY USE, helicopters had proven their worth for medical evacuation in the Korean War. However, the aircraft were still rare in the early 1950s, and the French in Indochina had few of them. What few they had, they used mainly for evacuating the wounded.

Castor. The French army had learned bloody lessons about the Viet Minh's ability to mass forces quickly and to react in overwhelming strength against an isolated or overextended enemy. Dien Bien Phu was clearly isolated. No help could come to the base by land. French army positions in the Red River delta and Laos were far away, over difficult terrain with few roads, and the Viet Minh could be counted on to attack any movement.

The air bridge concept was also risky. The long flying time from the delta to Dien Bien Phu limited the number of supply flights and the amount of supplies arriving at the base. The air bridge would also tie up much of the transport aircraft needed by other French forces. The French expected the coming seasonal rains to slow down Viet Minh supply efforts, but the same heavy rains could ground French supply flights to Dien Bien Phu and keep French aircraft from spotting and attacking the Viet Minh. The airfield was also vulnerable to Viet Minh artillery. If the Viet Minh managed to shut down the airstrip, the French would have to rely on supplies coming in by parachute.

Some officers also questioned whether the French at Dien Bien Phu could block Viet Minh movements and grind up attacking Viet Minh units. For an army that moved largely on foot, the Viet Minh had shown themselves to be highly mobile. They could reach and dominate northern Laos and other parts of the highlands by simply going around the valley. Rather than be caught in a French "meat grinder," the Viet Minh could simply "refuse combat"—that is, disappear into the jungle and avoid a fight. There was no guarantee Giap would take Navarre's bait and attack the French outpost as he had at Na San.

But if he did, the gamble could go terribly wrong. What if Giap raised the stakes and committed all his forces and resources to Dien Bien Phu? Viet Minh numbers and firepower could overwhelm the defenders one outlying position at a time.

Navarre overrode his officers' objections. The air bridge would work, he believed. The United States had already given the French additional aircraft and was about to commit more, along with support personnel. The French artillery commander, Colonel Charles Piroth, assured the planners that his forces could destroy the source of any Viet Minh shelling with their 105-millimeter and 155-millimeter howitzers. Fighter-bombers flying from Dien Bien Phu's airstrip could also silence enemy artillery positions and blunt attacks with bombs and machine-gun fire. The French could even fly in tanks to support their infantry.

War or Diplomacy?

Despite Navarre's enthusiasm for the coming battle, the priorities of the French government in Paris were changing. In fact, the political situation in Asia and the world had changed. Soviet dictator Joseph Stalin—blamed by many Western leaders for promoting the international expansion of Communism—died in March 1953, easing East–West tensions. The Korean War had settled into a military stalemate roughly along the 38th parallel, where U.S. firepower had stopped Chinese forces. In July 1953, North Korea, China, and the United Nations agreed to an armistice, or halt to combat. (The South Korean government refused to sign an agreement that left Korea divided.) The Chinese also indicated that they were interested in reducing tensions in Asia.

As for Indochina, French leaders wanted the military to simply hold on and keep its forces intact while looking for an opportunity to negotiate a way out of Vietnam. But Navarre had different ideas. Perhaps he thought that by going on the offensive, protecting Laos, and mauling the Viet Minh's divisions, he could improve France's bargaining position in future negotiations. He believed that Dien Bien Phu was the place to accomplish all this.

OPERATION CASTOR

Detailed planning for Operation Castor moved ahead. After elite airborne units cleared out any Viet Minh opposition at Dien Bien Phu, engineers and equipment would arrive by parachute. The engineers would expand the small airfield with steel matting. (The Viet Minh, with their usual attention to detail, had dug holes in the old grass strip to prevent landings.)

The repaired and improved airfield was the key. It would allow the French to quickly build up enough firepower to resist any Viet Minh attack and to develop a base from which French forces could range into the surrounding highlands, putting the Viet Minh off balance and keeping them from overrunning nearby Laos.

Navarre ordered the launch of Operation Castor on November

20, 1953. On the morning of the attack, veteran paratroopers, under the command of General Jean Gilles, waited at airfields in the delta. To maintain secrecy, commanders had not told the troops their destination. French officers directing Operation Castor flew above Dien Bien Phu, anxiously watching a ground mist covering the valley. Finally, the morning sun burned through the mist, and word went back to the airfields. Operation Castor was on.

The waiting paratroopers stubbed out their cigarettes. Weighed down and made bulky by their parachutes and gear, they slowly filed into the C-47 transport planes that would take them to the drop zone, twenty-five men to a plane. The paratroopers were no strangers to action, and they knew that for some it would be their last jump. One by one, the C-47s lifted off and headed west for the highlands.

IN THE 1950S, THE FRENCH USED C-47 TRANSPORT PLANES LIKE THESE TO DROP TROOPS AND SUPPLIES INTO VIETNAM.

As the Tai villagers in the valley went about their morning chores, soldiers from Viet Minh units were resting, training, and doing chores of their own. The initial single aircraft circling far above did not bother them. Then the first wave of C-47s came over the valley rim. The aircraft steadied their approach, and parachutes opened behind and below them. The Viet Minh knew what to expect. They trained their weapons on the descending paratroopers and opened fire.

The first paratroopers to land had to immediately fight off the Viet Minh. Some were killed even as they descended. The drop scattered paras up and down the valley. Once landed, individuals tried to join with groups of other paratroopers.

Major Marcel Bigeard, a legend in the parachute units, was able to organize a defense and communicate with other units and with Hanoi by radio. He was also able to call down machine-gun and napalm attacks from circling French aircraft to support his troops. The situation improved when Bigeard launched an attack to clear the Viet Minh from the drop zone. Another unit parachuted in. Soon the paras held the valley. They settled in for a long night in the highland cold, waiting with weapons at the ready for a Viet Minh counterattack.

The next day saw a steady stream of materials and reinforcing units dropped into the valley. General Gilles parachuted in and took command, riding around the valley on a tiny motor scooter that had been dropped in for his use. Air crews pushed some material, such as rolls of barbed wire, out of cargo aircraft, letting them free-fall into specified areas. Other equipment descended by parachute, not always with the best results. A bulldozer needed for work on the airfield broke free of its parachute lines and crashed into the drop zone, a useless wreck.

Within a few days, roughly five thousand men defended the drop zone. Light aircraft landed on the repaired airstrip while engineers

A French unit at Dien Bien Phu honors its dead in 1953.

expanded the field for heavier cargo aircraft. The French commander of the Tonkin region, General René Cogny, arrived to see the situation firsthand. Cogny was concerned that his chief, Navarre, had committed too many valuable units to the operation—units that Cogny needed to defend the Red River delta area. In addition, Cogny and Navarre had very different styles of leadership and at times seemed to dislike each other.

Giap Makes His Move

Far to the northeast, in his concealed headquarters near the Chinese border, General Giap received reports on the French buildup at Dien Bien Phu. The situation was promising. Giap had worried about the French trying to provoke the Viet Minh into an action closer to the delta, where French forces were stronger. Instead, they had chosen to set up a vulnerable position at Dien Bien Phu. Giap felt confident that he could determine the time, pace, and scale of the fighting that would follow. He knew better than to congratulate himself on his luck, however. He knew that only careful timing, skilled planning, and relentless willpower could turn that luck into victory.

Giap began moving his divisions toward Dien Bien Phu. The veteran 308th Division arrived to spearhead the encirclement of the

VIET MINH GENERAL VO NGUYEN GIAP *(IN BLACK)* TALKS WITH HIS AIDES IN 1954 AS THEY STUDY A MILITARY MAP.

French garrison, followed by the 312th Division. The 351st Division and its priceless artillery began to move toward the valley.

Most of the Viet Minh's movements went undetected by patrolling French aircraft. The Viet Minh were experts at camouflage. On their helmets and uniforms, they wore foliage from the areas they were passing through. They carefully screened equipment, heavy weapons, artillery, and rest areas with netting and foliage. They masked air-defense artillery at key sites along the roads, providing a nasty surprise for attacking French aircraft.

Moving Viet Minh forces toward Dien Bien Phu was a staggering logistical effort. Endless lines of porters moved along the trails, often relaying loads from one trail section to the next. Political education officers kept up the spirits of porters and troops. Labor battalions and engineers repaired and improved the roads to accommodate vehicles. Along the roads, trucks pulled artillery pieces—the centerpiece of Giap's emerging strategy.

By some estimates, hundreds of thousands of Vietnamese were involved in supplying the Viet Minh. The French had dismissed the Viet Minh's ability to move adequate supplies through difficult country, but Giap knew that the Viet Minh's incredible supply effort was the key to victory.

THE FRENCH PREPARE

The French were busy completing their own buildup. The defense system was based on eight fortified positions in the valley, all of them with common French women's names. Huguette, Claudine, Elaine, and Dominique occupied the center of the valley around the airstrip. The valley's northern end was anchored by Gabrielle, with Beatrice to the northeast and Anne-Marie to the northwest. A few miles down the valley lay Isabelle, with its own artillery and small airstrip. Scattered through the valley were Tai villages, although many of the villagers had fled at the first sign of fighting.

The French at Dien Bien Phu got a new commander: Colonel Christian de Castries. Descended from a long line of career military men, de Castries had risen through the cavalry, the branch of the army that moves in motor vehicles (previously horses) and the traditional branch for aristocrats. Navarre thought that this background made de Castries a good choice to command mobile forces operating out of Dien Bien Phu.

FRENCH GENERAL CHRISTIAN DE CASTRIES BECAME COMMANDER AT DIEN BIEN PHU IN 1953.

The French surrounded their positions with barbed wire and land mines to slow any waves of Viet Minh infantry, so that French firepower could mow them down. The French artillery commander, Colonel Piroth, boasted that his guns would devastate attacking infantry and silence any Viet Minh artillery firing on Dien Bien Phu.

Troops continued to arrive, including the famed Thirteenth Half-Brigade of the Foreign Legion. The Dien Bien Phu garrison was a microcosm of France's colonial army, with Senegalese from Africa,

FRENCH SOLDIERS DEFEND THEIR POSITION AT DIEN BIEN PHU. AS THEY BUILT UP THEIR DEFENSES, THE VIET MINH ALSO BROUGHT TROOPS AND WEAPONS INTO POSITION.

hardy Algerian and Moroccan riflemen, and Vietnamese from French units or the new Vietnamese National Army (in theory, in the service of Bao Dai's government but in fact commanded by the French).

The French flew in a small number of fighter-bomber and observation aircraft. Because the fighter-bombers could use the airfield to refuel and rearm, they could respond instantly to calls for air support. Missions flown from delta airfields took much longer to arrive and conduct. The French also brought in ten M-24 U.S. light tanks. Each tank arrived in two sections, and mechanics joined them on the spot.

As the Dien Bien Phu base was built up and Viet Minh forces arrived to surround it, the French sought more U.S. help. In particular, the French wanted more C-119 "Flying Boxcar" cargo aircraft and crews to fly and maintain them.

SIGNS OF TROUBLE

The French buildup at Dien Bien Phu continued into December. Meanwhile, French patrols pushing through tangled cover in the hills

THE FRENCH WANTED THE UNITED STATES TO GIVE THEM MORE C-119 "FLYING BOXCAR" CARGO AIRCRAFT TO USE IN THE WAR. THIS C-119 DROPS SUPPLIES TO U.S. TROOPS DURING THE KOREAN WAR IN 1951.

surrounding the valley encountered ominous signs of Viet Minh activity, such as well-built bunkers and trench systems. Viet Minh units were clearly present in strength. The Viet Minh often responded in force to French movements outside the fortified camp—another worrying sign.

The troops at Dien Bien Phu knew they were surrounded. Was their "hedgehog" turning into a deadly trap instead of a dagger pointed at the heart of the Viet Minh?

At the end of December, General Navarre ordered secret plans drawn up for a worst-case scenario. The plans included sending a force overland to rescue the Dien Bien Phu garrison and an emergency breakout of the French force if it was about to be overwhelmed. Neither idea was practical given the distances to French-controlled territory and the likelihood of ambush by entire Viet Minh divisions. Holding out really was the only hope.

With each week that passed, the French high command knew its position at Dien Bien Phu was more threatened. The French had intercepted Viet Minh orders for supplies and ammunition to be sent to Dien Bien Phu. General Cogny showed the orders to Navarre. They included a request for large quantities of antiaircraft ammunition—a bad omen for the safety of the French air bridge. French intelligence reports on the movement of Viet Minh units and the approach of the Viet Minh road and trail system indicated that the Viet Minh were seeking a showdown at Dien Bien Phu. Some in the French high command still believed that drawing the Viet Minh into a battle similar to Na San would bring a French victory. So far, though, the Viet Minh had not launched their expected massive attack.

U.S. Advice

BY 1954 U.S. POLITICIANS and military leaders were paying close attention to the situation in Vietnam. They had good reasons for concern. The United States was by then paying up to 80 percent of the cost of the French war. The United States had provided many of the aircraft, river vessels, tanks, and trucks used by the French. Americans wanted some say in how the money and material they were giving the French were used. To monitor French use of U.S. equipment, the United States had sent a small number of personnel to Vietnam, the Military Assistance Advisory Group, in 1950, but the French resisted any hint of U.S. interference in their operations.

In November 1953, "Iron Mike" O'Daniel, commander of U.S. Army forces in the Pacific, visited the French high command in Vietnam. He offered ideas on how to defend the Tonkin region and how to train the new Vietnamese National Army. The French listened politely but coolly to the U.S. general. O'Daniel returned uninvited in late January 1954 and suggested actions that the French knew had no chance of success. The French command, which had more urgent concerns, again brushed him off. In April 1954, O'Daniel became head of the U.S Military Assistance Advisory Group and helped the United States begin a closer involvement in Vietnamese affairs.

CHAPTER 7

The Noose Tightens

URING JANUARY AND FEBRUARY 1954, both sides
at Dien Bien Phu continued to build up their forces and probe
each other's positions. The situation was clearly turning into a siege—a
campaign in which one force (the Viet Minh) surrounds the other (the
French). The Viet Minh began digging in around the French emplacements so that—at least by land—no supplies could get in and no
French forces could get out. Both sides prepared for a showdown.

Some supplies and men still reached the valley via the French air
bridge, but the French had overestimated the volume the air route
could safely deliver. The pace and volume of the Viet Minh supply
effort had no such limitations. Fresh Viet Minh units continued to
arrive and take positions around the valley. Hundreds of troops pulled,
dragged, and pushed each all-important artillery piece to its position,
unseen by the French.

Sidetracks

TWO DISTRACTIONS TO THE Dien Bien Phu operations took place in January 1954. Early in the month, French paratroop units moved to Laos to stop a surprise Viet Minh thrust, intended by Giap to draw off French resources. The French high command also divided its own resources by launching Operation Atlante at the end of January. The operation landed troops to link with other forces on the coast of central Vietnam to help clear the Viet Minh out of the central region. The operation showed very poor results because the Viet Minh once again simply refused combat in the face of the large French force.

Giap followed his own timetable. Not ready to attack until all his artillery was in place, he sent units on diversionary attacks into Laos while reinforcing his encirclement of the French and ratcheting up the pressure on French positions.

At the end of January, Giap opened a new phase in the siege by using his artillery. At first the shelling on French positions was light. The French interpreted this level of shelling to mean that the Viet Minh had not brought up much artillery or that French counter-battery fire had reduced or intimidated the artillery. But in fact, with the occasional shelling, the Viet Minh were sighting in their guns from the heights above the valley and testing French responses.

On February 3, the Viet Minh gave a hint of their massed firepower with a barrage of 75-millimeter fire on French positions. The French responded with artillery and air strikes. Much of the French response was wasted, however. The Viet Minh had cleverly made fake emplacements with log "gun barrels" projecting from them. The French shelled these easy targets and left the real artillery untouched.

As if realizing their oversight too late, the French at Dien Bien Phu tried to improve their position by taking high ground around the valley. A sweep in February cleared the Viet Minh off some hills at the cost of many casualties, but the French lacked the troop strength to hold the hills.

Moving through the tangled jungle and along steep slopes left French soldiers exhausted and sometimes bloody, but they seldom caught the Viet Minh by surprise. Returning to camp, French soldiers

FRENCH AND VIETNAMESE TROOPS SEARCH THE WOODED AREA AROUND DIEN BIEN PHU FOR VIET MINH FORCES IN 1954.

had to resume the tiresome work of digging their own trenches and bunkers, by then a way of life at Dien Bien Phu. It was hard to maintain morale in such circumstances. Some soldiers deserted.

Soldiers in the fortified camp lived as best as they could. They drank purified water from the muddy Nam Yum River, which flowed down the valley. They sometimes mixed the water with Vinogel, a sort of thickened wine. Rations were basic. Cooks did their best to feed the troops and to cater to different nationalities and their various dietary requirements. Most of France's North African troops, for example, practiced the Islamic religion, which prohibited them from eating pork.

Medical facilities and treatment at Dien Bien Phu were limited. Medical teams had been flown in, and as long as aircraft could land, the badly wounded could be flown out on evacuation flights. A surgical center and other facilities were buried in deep bunkers, and preparations were made to handle casualties from large attacks. Some wondered if these preparations would be enough. What would happen if shelling closed the airfield?

Spot On

ARTILLERY UNITS GENERALLY FIRE howitzers, which lob their shells in a high arc, from behind the crests of hills—safe from return fire. But the Viet Minh at Dien Bien Phu took a different approach. They positioned their howitzers on the forward slopes of hills, facing the enemy, and protected them inside deep shelters dug into the hillsides and expertly concealed by camouflage. With this arrangement, Giap's gunners could aim directly at their targets in the valley.

THE BIG PICTURE

Far from the battlefield, at a meeting in Berlin, West Germany, in February 1954, the governments of France, Great Britain, the United States, and the Soviet Union agreed to hold an international conference to deal with the conflicts in Korea and Vietnam. The conference was to be held in Geneva, Switzerland, in April of that year.

Both French and Viet Minh leaders immediately realized the connection between the upcoming conference and their military situation. For each side, a victory at Dien Bien Phu would greatly strengthen its bargaining position. Both forces knew they had to avoid disaster, and both realized that timing was vital. With the cream of the French army in Indochina surrounded at Dien Bien Phu, however, it was Giap's Viet Minh forces who had the advantage, and Giap intended to press it.

The Chinese had their own ideas about the upcoming battle. Mao Zedong's Communist government had given Giap a large group of advisers. They assisted Viet Minh units with training, advice on tactics, and technical needs—and worked closely in the field with howitzer and antiaircraft units. Throughout the winter, Chinese advisers pressured Giap to mount human wave assaults to annihilate French positions. But Giap had taken such advice in the past and lost thousands of men in failed attacks. This time he held to his own more cautious timetable. Giap also resisted calls from some in the Viet Minh leadership to use Chinese troops more widely in combat—which might give the Chinese more influence over Vietnam. Giap felt it was better for the Viet Minh to do their own fighting.

FROM SIEGE TO BATTLE

By early March, Viet Minh 75-millimeter guns were routinely shelling the French airfield. The shells tore up the steel matting of the runway and hit some aircraft. Disrupting the air bridge was a priority for the Viet Minh, who sent commandos at night to destroy more of the runway and to blow up French aircraft on airfields back in the delta.

Giap began using his 105-millimeter howitzers to blast any aircraft remaining on the strip. By then the Viet Minh had surrounded

Giap's Guns

THE VIET MINH ARTILLERY was crucial to success on the battlefield, and much of it originated in the United States. U.S. equipment provided to French and Chinese Nationalist armies during and after World War II and from the battlefields of Korea ended up blasting French hopes at Dien Bien Phu.

U.S.-made guns included 105-millimeter howitzers, captured by Chinese Communist armies in Korea and funneled to the Viet Minh. The 105s packed a big punch. They were designed to be towed behind a truck and operated by a crew of several soldiers. The Viet Minh also had U.S.-made 75-millimeter "pack" howitzers, which could be broken down into parts and carried on the backs of animals (or by Viet Minh porters). Kept light for airborne or mountain units, the 75s were less powerful than the 105s.

Rounding out the Viet Minh artillery force were 120-millimeter mortars (not necessarily from the United States), which threw heavy shells on a high arc. The Viet Minh also had Soviet-model 37-millimeter antiaircraft guns and 12.7-millimeter heavy machine guns that could bring down aircraft. Infantry units were well equipped with smaller mortars.

the French camp with a network of trenches. The Viet Minh became masters of siege warfare. They worked in teams to dig small trenches toward the French lines. These trenches protected Viet Minh units moving up to attack.

French intelligence predicted a major Viet Minh attack for March 15. On March 12, General Cogny paid a quick visit to the entrenched French camp. He encouraged the defenders, but everything pointed to the siege entering a new and more violent phase. By then shelling had destroyed several aircraft. It was clear that the vital airfield might not remain open much longer.

The storm broke on the afternoon of March 13. At five in the afternoon, a massive Viet Minh artillery barrage fell on French positions. The French had left their artillery in the open, instead of dug in, so that they could fire in any direction. The Viet Minh artillery barrage rained down on the exposed guns and crews, blowing them apart and preventing them from firing in response.

The bombardment was like nothing the French had seen before in Vietnam. The Viet Minh concentrated artillery fire on French positions and lobbed in mortar shells. Covered by artillery, the Viet Minh pushed their attack trenches to the French lines and brought up recoilless rifles and light mortars for supporting fire. Viet Minh advance parties blew open passages through barbed wire with explosive charges pushed under the wire on long poles. Then the Viet Minh swarmed up from their trenches to attack.

The Foreign Legion defenders holding the strongpoint Beatrice were hit hard. Wave after wave of Viet Minh attackers raced into the post. Some threw satchel charges (high explosives in bags) into bunkers. The Viet Minh had rehearsed their attacks with models of the fortifications and knew exactly where to go.

French artillery and mortars firing from other positions took a toll on the Beatrice attackers, but the very accurate Viet Minh shelling did far more damage to the French positions. Shells hit ammunition and fuel stocks and blasted command posts, killing senior officers. Casualties swamped French aid stations, and the senior French surgeon, Major Paul Grauwin, operated nonstop. Outside the central medical station, French soldiers piled up the bodies of those who could not be saved.

On Beatrice the defenders fought fiercely to hold their positions, in the best tradition of the Foreign Legion. A final wave of Viet Minh

MEMBERS OF THE MEDICAL CORPS CARRY WOUNDED FRENCH SOLDIERS FROM A HELICOPTER DURING THE BATTLE OF DIEN BIEN PHU IN 1954.

infantry overwhelmed the defenders, and the French lost radio contact. Some Legionnaires managed to slip out of Beatrice into nearby French positions, but more lay dead or terribly wounded on the rise they had defended at such cost.

In an unusual gesture, the morning after the Beatrice attack, the Viet Minh allowed a short truce so that the French could collect their dead and wounded. When the truce ended, Viet Minh artillery fire pounded the central camp and airstrip. French planes dropped reinforcements—a parachute battalion of the Vietnamese National Army, along with a desperately needed surgical team. French ground crews were able to ready a few fighter-bombers, which took off into the teeth of Viet Minh shellfire and escaped. Other French aircraft were destroyed.

A FRENCH MILITARY HELICOPTER FLIES OVERHEAD AS FRENCH SOLDIERS TRY TO DEFEND THEIR POSITION AT DIEN BIEN PHU IN MARCH 1954.

The Viet Minh's next target was Gabrielle, a hill at the top of the roughly T-shaped French camp system in the valley. A unit of seasoned Algerian riflemen held the position. They had seen the devastation rained on Beatrice and braced for an attack. A mass of shells fell on the position, stunning the defenders. Then Viet Minh troops swarmed toward the Algerians. The Algerians fought back with everything they had, turning flamethrowers on the Viet Minh and bayoneting those who got close enough.

After a lull, during which Giap replaced the exhausted attackers with a fresh unit, Viet Minh artillery fire intensified. It wiped out the command post for Gabrielle. At dawn the French launched a counterattack to relieve Gabrielle. But when relief troops reached the position, they found Algerian defenders abandoning Gabrielle because of a misunderstood order. The French had no choice but to retreat and abandon Gabrielle to the arriving Viet Minh.

The French had lost two of their eight positions in as many days. A sad note was added by the suicide of Colonel Piroth, the French artillery commander. Contrary to his boasts, Piroth's artillery could not silence the Viet Minh guns killing so many of his comrades. Devastated by his own misjudgment, he took his own life.

On March 16, new units parachuted into Dien Bien Phu to replace French losses and stiffen defenses. The new arrivals found the valley a blasted moonscape of trenches and shell craters. Morale was crumbling. Meanwhile, the Viet Minh had begun to distribute leaflets to Tai soldiers holding the Anne-Marie position. The leaflets encouraged the Tai to desert rather than serve the French colonialists. Dazed by shelling and swayed by this propaganda, the Tai soldiers fled into the jungle. Another strongpoint was lost.

FRENCH PARATROOPERS DROP INTO DIEN BIEN PHU IN MARCH 1954 TO HELP DEFEND THE BATTERED GARRISON.

From Gabrielle and Anne-Marie, the Viet Minh turned the brunt of their fire on the airstrip. Antiaircraft guns constantly fired on evacuation flights as they tried to land or to take off with the wounded.

French pilots flew countless missions trying to silence the Viet Minh guns. Finally, the French turned to the Americans for help. The United States provided C-119 transport aircraft, which the French rigged to drop napalm bombs on hillside gun emplacements. The French unleashed the napalm attacks at the end of March but could not burn out enough artillery positions to stop the shelling that was making the airstrip unusable.

The last act was approaching for the garrison of Dien Bien Phu. It was to be a prolonged and tortured end.

CHAPTER 8

Endgame

BY THE END OF MARCH, the situation for the French at
Dien Bien Phu was grim. The scale of their strategic and tacti-
cal blunders was becoming apparent to the French high command.
France knew it faced defeat—the only question was how badly it
would lose. Even if a rescue were feasible, few French units could
be spared to help Dien Bien Phu. The only real hope for the French
seemed to lie in the United States coming to the rescue.

U.S. president Dwight Eisenhower and his secretary of state, John
Foster Dulles, were concerned about Communist expansion in Asia,
but they sent mixed signals to the French about possible U.S. support. The Eisenhower administration did not want Vietnam to fall to
Communism, but the United States was already paying a big percentage of France's war bill and was not convinced that more money and
equipment were the answer.

The Domino Theory

PRESIDENT DWIGHT EISENHOWER and other U.S. leaders used an interesting metaphor to explain the advance of Communism through the world. They imagined a row of dominoes—flat, rectangular game pieces—standing on their edges. In 1954 Eisenhower explained, "You have a row of dominoes set up, you knock over the first one, and what will happen to the last one is the certainty that it will go over very quickly. So you could have. . . the loss of Indochina, of Burma, of Thailand, of the Peninsula, and Indonesia." In other words, Eisenhower believed that if one nation fell to Communism, nearby nations would quickly fall as well.

LOSING THE BATTLE

Back in Dien Bien Phu, French forces tenaciously defended their shrinking perimeter. The commander, de Castries, seemed to be losing touch with the situation. He became depressed and withdrawn and allowed the paratroop leader, Colonel Pierre Langlais, to direct operations.

Viet Minh antiaircraft guns were still endangering medical evacuation flights and were forcing supply missions to drop their loads from high altitudes—making the delivery of supplies increasingly inaccurate. French paras, under the command of Major Marcel Bigeard, were able to destroy some of the guns. The mission showed what aggressive action could do, but it resulted in many casualties and exhausted valuable troops.

Meanwhile, a network of freshly dug Viet Minh trenches advanced toward the shrinking French camp. The seasonal rains began, nearly filling some of the French fortifications. A foul, muddy swamp, including rotting corpses and human waste, oozed into the French positions.

VIET MINH SOLDIERS SIT IN A TRENCH NEAR DIEN BIEN PHU IN 1954. THE TRENCHES WERE IMPORTANT FOR THE VIET MINH IN THEIR DEFEAT OF THE FRENCH MILITARY.

On March 30, fighting raged for control of Dominique and Elaine. Under pressure from massed Viet Minh assaults, soldiers in French North African units on Dominique fled their positions. Waves of Viet Minh attackers seized part of Elaine and threatened to swarm into the rest of the French camp. The French fired 105-millimeter howitzers into the approaching Viet Minh, and Algerian riflemen made a stubborn stand, which turned the tide. The next day, French and Vietnamese paras counterattacked and retook lost ground but then had to yield it to superior Viet Minh numbers.

The French not only had to fight off Viet Minh assaults. If they lost ground overlooking the airfield and what was left of their camp, they had to retake it immediately, before the Viet Minh could settle in. Both sides were locked in a pitiless infantry battle of mass assaults and desperate counterattacks, but the French forces had no chance of relief. Exhausted and bled in the grinder of Dien Bien Phu, French forces were running out of nearly everything they needed to fight. Ammunition for the artillery was in very short supply. When air-dropped, some ammunition landed behind enemy lines, and the Viet Minh used it against the French.

The Legion Lives On

FRANCE CREATED THE FOREIGN LEGION in the 1830s. Consisting of foreign soldiers, the legion took part in many French colonial wars. Foreign Legion units fought stubbornly at Dien Bien Phu—and suffered heavily. The Foreign Legion later participated in peacekeeping missions and military interventions in Africa. The Foreign Legion still serves France in the twenty-first century. It is stationed in the African nation of Djibouti.

FRENCH SOLDIERS RETURN FIRE AROUND THE GARRISON AT DIEN
BIEN PHU. AT THE END OF THE SIEGE, THE SOLDIERS WERE UNDER
CONSTANT ATTACK FROM VIET MINH FORCES.

On the last day of March, the Viet Minh launched a massive assault on Huguette. A unit of French-led Vietnamese paras drove out
the attackers, but by this time, General Navarre could only plan for
the end. The choices were stark.

The weakened garrison, slowed by its wounded, had no hope of fighting its way back to French lines over rugged country, so a breakout attempt was out of the question. It would have resulted in a massacre. Prideful General Navarre would not hear of surrender. He could only promise reinforcements and urge de Castries to hold on as long as possible. He also gave secret orders to destroy French equipment if the Viet Minh overran the entire camp.

EISENHOWER THINKS TWICE

By early April, leaders in Washington, D.C., were discussing reports on the worsening situation at Dien Bien Phu. The United States and France began planning in secret to unleash Operation Vulture, a massive bombing of Viet Minh positions by U.S. B-29 bombers. The French government also asked the Eisenhower administration for a strike by U.S. carrier-based aircraft. Some accounts claim that the United States offered to use nuclear weapons to clear out the Viet Minh or to provide nuclear weapons to the French.

The U.S. president remained cautious. Eisenhower knew the realities of power better than most leaders. As leader of the Allied forces in Europe during World War II, he had commanded the largest military alliance in history. As president of the United States, he had helped bring the Korean War to a negotiated close. U.S. troops were already stretched thin around the world, and propping up the French in Vietnam would require a major commitment of forces. Senior generals warned Eisenhower that direct U.S. military involvement in Vietnam could expand greatly once it begun. What if the Chinese intervened on the side of the Viet Minh? According to some reports, Chinese crews were already operating antiaircraft guns at Dien Bien Phu. The next step

could easily be masses of Chinese infantry pouring across the border.

In secret briefings, the Eisenhower administration presented its options to the congressional leadership. The leaders, including Senator Lyndon Johnson (later U.S. president), objected to the United States acting alone to prop up French rule but would consider it if Great Britain offered help. But British prime minister Winston Churchill did not want to involve Great Britain in a war that could draw in China and even the nuclear-armed Soviet Union.

U.S. PRESIDENT DWIGHT EISENHOWER SENT HELP TO THE FRENCH DURING THE BATTLE OF DIEN BIEN PHU.

Despite the risks, the Americans kept their options open, sending two aircraft carriers to the Gulf of Tonkin off the coast of northern Vietnam. The United States also supported the French effort by providing hundreds of noncombat personnel and rushing delivery of urgently needed items such as napalm and parachutes.

THE VALLEY OF SUFFERING

Inside the French lines at Dien Bien Phu, fewer and fewer men were able to fight. The defenders fell to shelling and sniper fire. On April

10, the French overcame fierce resistance and drove the Viet Minh from a part of Elaine they had previously seized. Such counterattacks cost the French more casualties, which they could not replace. The wounded were jammed into medical aid stations under filthy conditions. Short on supplies, doctors treated them the best they could. Some wounded troops even volunteered to return to fight with their comrades.

The Viet Minh continued to distribute leaflets among French units. The messages urged Vietnamese, North African, and western African troops to desert the French—their colonial oppressors—and some did. A few deserters surrendered to the Viet Minh. Others, fearful of surrendering, dug caves into the banks of a river and scavenged for air-dropped food.

The battle entered its desperate final act. Viet Minh units surrounded the strongpoint Isabelle, completely cutting it off and massing to attack. At Huguette the Viet Minh wiped out a Foreign Legion unit making a last stand. Giap urged his men to keep up their morale, to keep up the pressure on the enemy, and kill as many French troops as possible.

The French defenders of Dien Bien Phu kept up their own spirits only with hopes of a rescue. But they did not know the reality of the situation: all the French could put together was an understrength rescue column advancing from Laos. It had little chance of fighting its way through to Dien Bien Phu. And hopes for a U.S. rescue were dashed when President Eisenhower declared on April 27 that the United States would not act militarily on its own in Vietnam.

Planning began for a breakout by French forces—a move that would require the French to leave the badly wounded behind. De Castries kept the plan secret for fear of demoralizing his troops.

LAST STAND

Back at Dien Bien Phu, the Viet Minh celebrated May Day (May 1), the international workers' holiday, with a massive artillery bombardment. Viet Minh infantry assaults overwhelmed French positions on Elaine, Dominique, and Huguette. The French lost more positions in the next few days, often with a handful of defenders fighting to the death against thousands of Viet Minh troops. French forces could by then hear the sounds of the Viet Minh tunneling under their positions, either preparing to attack or placing explosives to blow up French strongpoints.

De Castries sent out desperate demands for more of everything—men, supplies, and ammunition. The last reinforcements to arrive were fewer than one hundred paras, who jumped into Dien Bien Phu on May 6. On the same day, James McGovern and Wallace Bufford, U.S. civilian pilots hired to fly supplies to Dien Bien Phu, were shot down by Viet Minh antiaircraft fire. McGovern and Bufford are sometimes cited as the first U.S. deaths in the Vietnam conflict.

Giap began the final push on the night of May 6. The French beat back mass assaults, with hundreds of Viet Minh dying, but the defenders' numbers were dwindling fast. The Viet Minh exploded a giant mine under a position on Elaine, but a handful of survivors there stopped a Viet Minh infantry rush. As depleted French units shifted to cover widening holes in the defense, other units made their last stands. Before being overwhelmed by waves of Viet Minh, French officers destroyed their radios so that the enemy could not use them or listen in on their frequencies. The French lost contact with position after position.

Late in the afternoon of May 7, de Castries spoke by radio with the commander of operations in northern Vietnam, General Cogny in Hanoi. To preserve the honor of France and the French units at Dien Bien Phu, Cogny ordered de Castries not to surrender but instead to destroy all usable war materials and to cease resistance. The generals made their good-byes. This was the last radio transmission from French-held Dien Bien Phu.

SOME OF THE LAST FRENCH TROOPS AT DIEN BIEN PHU WAIT IN TRENCHES BUILT AROUND THE GARRISON ON MAY 7, 1954.

The defenders of Dien Bien Phu had fought to the end with honor against incredible odds. For those who survived the siege, Dien Bien Phu had indeed been hell. Then came the ordeal of captivity.

PRISONERS

As resistance died down, Viet Minh troops swarmed over the French positions. Viet Minh soldiers cautiously entered the trenches and bunkers and herded surrendering French troops out in groups. The Viet Minh were anxious to get the prisoners out of reach of possible French rescue attempts. The captors and their nearly eleven thousand prisoners began a long march to jungle camps hundreds of miles away.

On the trail, the Viet Minh relentlessly pushed the prisoners—weakened from months of combat and hard living. Once they reached camp, the Viet Minh subjected prisoners to a brainwashing campaign. They lectured prisoners on the error of fighting for the cause of colonialism and imperialism. They singled out the North Africans for intense propaganda against continuing French rule of their homelands. Vietnamese troops in the French forces underwent "reeducation," consisting of pro-Communist and anti-imperialist lectures, harsh punishments, and rewards for renouncing their support of the puppet government headed by Bao Dai.

For the Viet Minh, the prisoners would be a valuable bargaining tool in upcoming negotiations, so it was important to keep them alive. Yet many prisoners suffered from diseases contracted at Dien Bien Phu or along the trail. Many died on the road or after arriving at prison camps. In the end, fewer than one-third of the Dien Bien Phu prisoners survived captivity.

GUARDED BY VIET MINH SOLDIERS, FRENCH SOLDIERS CAPTURED AFTER THE FALL OF DIEN BIEN PHU MARCH TO A PRISON CAMP IN MAY 1954.

From his headquarters, General Navarre soberly took stock of the French situation in Vietnam. He realized that as soon as the Viet Minh moved their divisions from Dien Bien Phu to menace the Red River delta, he would be hard-pressed to defend the heartland around Hanoi and Haiphong. At Dien Bien Phu, he had lost much of his mobile reserve—the airborne troops he needed to move quickly to trouble spots. Militarily, France had little choice but to negotiate as graceful a way out of Vietnam as possible.

The Last to Die:
The Destruction of Groupe Mobile 100

EARLY IN 1954, THE French landed troops by sea and moved forces into central Vietnam to challenge Viet Minh dominance of the area. The French forces moved inland and established control of roads and fortified camps in Vietnam's central plateau.

After the fall of Dien Bien Phu, the French command was anxious to extract its forces from the central region and avoid another disaster. In June and July, a force called Groupe Mobile 100 went in to evacuate isolated French outposts and move remaining garrisons back toward the coast along the area's routes colonials.

A series of Viet Minh ambushes turned the mission into a bloodbath. The Viet Minh nearly wiped out entire French units, including veteran French battalions that had fought alongside the Americans in Korea. They would be some of the last French forces to die in Indochina. A few days after the dazed survivors made it to safety, the participants at the Geneva Conference agreed on an immediate cease-fire.

WORLD REACTION

In France and around the world, people reacted to the fall of Dien Bien Phu with shock and amazement. The reality was that the Viet Minh at Dien Bien Phu had fielded a well-trained army that greatly outnumbered French forces and, thanks to Chinese help, was in some ways better equipped. Nonetheless, it appeared as though a band of ragged revolutionaries had humbled a major colonial power. In Asian countries only recently free or still freeing themselves from European colonial rule, the Viet Minh victory brought pride. In the North African countries of Tunisia, Morocco, and Algeria, which were controlled by France, the Viet Minh triumph helped inspire independence movements.

In France the mood was grim. Many Western Europeans and Americans were also downhearted. They saw the loss at Dien Bien Phu as a worrying sign of the advance of Communism around the world. Although it had been unwilling to rescue the French at Dien Bien Phu, the Eisenhower administration stressed the need to contain further Communist advances in Asia. U.S. attention shifted toward blocking Communist interests at the Geneva Conference.

THE GENEVA ACCORDS

On May 8, the participants in Geneva finally turned their attention to Indochina. The parties at the negotiations were the French-controlled governments of Laos, Cambodia, and Bao Dai's Associated State of Vietnam, along with France and the Democratic Republic of Vietnam (the Viet Minh). The Soviet Union, China, Great Britain, and the United States contributed their weight as major powers. The real movers behind the conference were Britain's foreign secretary, Anthony Eden, and the new French prime minister, Pierre Mendes-France. Mendes-France openly declared his intention to reach a quick agreement on Vietnam, while Eden helped keep the conference focused on the goal of improving relations between the Communist powers and the West.

The Viet Minh delegation was led by Pham Van Dong, a senior political leader. He knew that the Viet Minh victory at Dien Bien Phu would help his position in negotiations. He also knew that

PARTICIPANTS IN THE GENEVA CONFERENCE BEGAN DISCUSSING THE
SITUATION IN VIETNAM ON MAY 8, 1954. THIS PHOTOGRAPH SHOWS
DELEGATES FROM THE VIET MINH, FRANCE, AND THE ASSOCIATED
STATE OF VIETNAM.

success for the Viet Minh depended on the two heavyweight Communist powers at the conference—China and the Soviet Union.
But Dong was suspicious of their intentions. He suspected that
China, the Soviets, or both might betray the Viet Minh—and stop
short of demanding total independence for Vietnam to serve a
separate agenda.

After two months of haggling, conference participants arrived at a set of agreements known as the Geneva Accords. Under the accords, Vietnam became fully independent—although its government was yet to be determined. Laos and Cambodia also became fully independent states. The accords also stated that within three hundred days, Viet Minh forces were to move north of the 17th parallel (which split the country in two—North and South), while French and Associated State of Vietnam forces were to move south of that line. French forces would leave Indochina by 1956. An International Control Commission, made up of representatives from India, Poland, and Canada, would supervise the implementation of the agreement.

The arrangement also called for national elections, scheduled for July 1956, to determine the future government of Vietnam. The Viet Minh had hoped for a better deal. They wanted full control of Vietnam under their own Communist government. In some ways, the Geneva Accords cheated them of the full fruits of their battlefield victories. But the Chinese and especially the Soviets—who wished to improve relations with the West—pressured the Viet Minh to accept the agreement. Exhausted from years of fighting, the Viet Minh signed on to the accords. In any case, they expected to easily win the July 1956 elections.

Aware that an election would probably favor the Communists, the United States did not sign the final agreement. Instead, the United States signed a separate document stating that the United States "took notice" of the treaty provisions and would not use force to oppose treaty terms it disagreed with. More important, the United States persuaded Bao Dai to make Ngo Dinh Diem prime minister of the Associated State of Vietnam. A Catholic, Diem was

both anti-French and anti-Communist. He had worked in the United States and knew many influential Americans. The United States wanted him in charge in Vietnam.

The conference ended a partial success. The states of Indochina finally had their independence. France was allowed a graceful withdrawal from Vietnam. The eventual unification of Vietnam under the Communists seemed certain, and the United States was pleased that it was not bound by the terms of the Geneva Accords.

AT THE URGING OF THE UNITED STATES, NGO DINH DIEM (ABOVE) BECAME PRIME MINISTER OF VIETNAM IN 1954.

The Next French Fight

IN THE MID-TWENTIETH CENTURY, Algeria was an important French possession. French rule there dated to the mid-1800s, and the area was home to many French citizens. But, as in Vietnam, native Algerians resented French rule. An independence movement developed in Algeria. It turned violent in 1954. Two years later, in 1956, France granted independence to two other North African territories, Tunisia and Morocco, but it kept control of Algeria.

In the mid-1950s, as the Algerian independence movement grew stronger, France sent Foreign Legion and colonial units to put down the rebellion. Violence mounted between Algerian guerrillas on one side, and French colonists and the French army on the other.

French soldiers, some of them hardened Indochina War veterans, sometimes used brutality as they rooted out and suppressed Algerian independence fighters. Marcel Bigeard, a hero of Dien Bien Phu, led a French parachute regiment during the Battle of Algiers in 1957. Bigeard freely admitted that his men used torture to get information from the Algerians. Some witnesses even accused paras of throwing Algerian prisoners out of helicopters.

By 1960 casualties in the hundreds of thousands and brutal methods used by both sides had made the war unpopular in France. Meanwhile, generals and units bloodied in Indochina and angry at yet another betrayal by politicians tried unsuccessfully to overthrow the French government. Finally, weary of war, a majority of French citizens came to favor Algerian independence. After negotiating a cease-fire, Charles de Gaulle's government declared Algeria independent in July 1962.

CHAPTER 9

New Man in the South

A S THE FRENCH PREPARED to leave Indochina, the United States increasingly supported Ngo Dinh Diem. Meanwhile, a flood of mostly Catholic refugees began moving south from northern Vietnam. These people were afraid of living under Communism. A propaganda campaign, created by the U.S. Central Intelligence Agency, had fueled their fears—warning that the Viet Minh would suppress their religion and seize their property.

French and U.S. ships transported up to a million northerners to the South. These northerners provided their fellow Catholic Diem with a base of support, and he rewarded many of them with land and other benefits. At the same time, most Viet Minh forces in the South moved north of the 17th parallel, but Viet Minh leaders instructed many political organizers to stay behind. Therefore, large areas in the South remained under Viet Minh control.

Friends in High Places

BEFORE HE BECAME PRESIDENT of the Republic of Vietnam, Ngo Dinh Diem had already made important U.S. friends. Diem's brother was a Catholic bishop and a friend of the powerful cardinal Francis Spellman—an important Catholic leader in the United States. In the 1950s, Spellman arranged introductions for Diem to members of the U.S. political establishment, including then senator John F. Kennedy.

Diem managed to gain support of the Vietnamese army, despite the opposition of its commander, Nguyen Van Hinh, a French citizen who despised Diem. Diem also won the support of the private armies of the Cao Dai and Hoa Hao religious sects and moved against the forces of the Binh Xuyen gangsters who controlled much of Saigon.

With his position strengthened, Diem turned to his future role in Vietnam. He announced an October 1955 election, with voters choosing between himself and Bao Dai as Vietnam's head of state. He then put his brother in charge of the voting. Not surprisingly, Diem was able to claim that more than 98 percent of the vote was in his favor. In some districts, the number of votes for Diem far exceeded the number of eligible voters.

Diem then removed Bao Dai as head of government and proclaimed himself president of the newly named Republic of Vietnam, also called South Vietnam. In 1956 Diem announced that the South would not take part in elections planned for that year—elections that by the Geneva Accords were supposed to unify Vietnam under a single government. Diem claimed that the elections would not be conducted fairly in the North, so he canceled them in the South.

Diem was a sincere Vietnamese nationalist, but his instinct to protect his own power and advance his family's interests clouded his judgment. By favoring the new Catholic minority from the North and allowing his family members to become a corrupt ruling clique, Diem seemed out of touch with most South Vietnamese. But he knew he had to move soon against political opponents, Communists and non-Communists alike.

Diem and his siblings and other relatives proved to be ruthless. They had political opponents executed or imprisoned under harsh conditions on Con Son Island, where the French had kept Viet Minh prisoners. Diem also created a secret police force loyal to him and widely feared by citizens.

U.S. PRESIDENT DWIGHT EISENHOWER *(LEFT)* AND VIETNAM'S PRESIDENT NGO DINH DIEM *(RIGHT)* SHAKE HANDS IN WASHINGTON, D.C. LOOKING ON IS U.S. SECRETARY OF STATE JOHN FOSTER DULLES *(CENTER)*.

The French still had forces in the South. They saw Diem as an incompetent leader with bitterly anti-French views, and they worked to replace him. The United States, however, saw Diem as a defender of the "free world" and turned a blind eye to his excesses and abuses of power. For the United States, Diem was "our man" in Vietnam and the best hope for countering Communist expansion in Southeast Asia. The United States dramatically stepped up financial and military aid to Diem.

France and the United States had informal agreements that called for the United States to take over many of France's obligations in South Vietnam, such as education and government administration, but the French expected to maintain a presence as advisers and trainers in these areas. To their annoyance, the French found themselves quickly sidelined as U.S. military and civilian experts arrived in South Vietnam.

THE VIET CONG

U.S. hopes that Diem would stabilize the Republic of Vietnam as a barrier to Communism at first seemed to be coming true. Diem tried to root out Communist elements. The United States hoped that an association of anti-Communist nations formed in 1954, the Southeast Asia Treaty Organization (SEATO), would further help the region resist the advance of Communism.

From 1955 on, Diem grew more confident and his security apparatus became stronger. However, his favoritism toward Catholics angered Buddhists, who made up the majority of the South Vietnamese population. College students and other educated Vietnamese resented Diem's heavy-handed rule and his family's corruption.

Communist guerrillas within South Vietnam began violently challenging Diem's rule. These fighters were called Viet Cong—a shortened version of the Vietnamese term for "Vietnamese Communist." By 1957 the guerrillas had begun a terror campaign, assassinating government officials and even teachers in an effort to control the countryside. At first, however, the Viet Cong were too weak to undertake major operations and were under pressure from Diem's security forces.

Diem created laws and military courts to target suspected Communists and to punish protests against his regime. Even membership in a suspect organization could bring severe penalties, including execution. This repression only worsened the cycle of protests and violence. By opposing the dreaded Diem regime, the Communists attracted additional followers. Communist activities made Diem crack down all the harder. He came close to destroying the Communist apparatus in the South.

THE NORTH

The years after Dien Bien Phu and the Geneva Accords were difficult for the Democratic Republic of Vietnam, or North Vietnam as it came to be called. Ho Chi Minh's government tried to concentrate on rebuilding the country after years of war with the French. It made hasty and heavy-handed reforms, such as seizing farms from private landowners and redistributing the land to peasants—a classic policy in Communist regimes.

The North called repeatedly for the elections on national unification required by the Geneva Accords, but the South refused to cooperate. By the late 1950s, the leadership of North Vietnam had given up on reunifying Vietnam using political methods. Instead, the leaders decided to launch a guerrilla struggle in the South, supported and supplied from the North. The goal was to topple Diem's regime to clear the way for reunification under a Communist government. The North Vietnamese began to provide weapons to the Viet Cong in the South.

To further assist the Viet Cong, in 1959 the North Vietnamese ordered the development of a supply route from North to South. The Viet Minh's skillfully hidden system of roads and trails for bringing in supplies and weapons over jungle-clad mountains from China had been the key to victory at Dien Bien Phu. Drawing on this experience, the North Vietnamese built what the Americans came to call the Ho Chi Minh Trail.

NORTH VIETNAMESE TROOPS TRAVEL THE HO CHI MINH TRAIL. THE TRAIL WAS AN IMPORTANT SUPPLY ROUTE FOR THE NORTH VIETNAMESE DURING THE VIETNAM WAR.

Supplies moved from the southern part of North Vietnam along a network of parallel roads and secondary tracks. Most of the Ho Chi Minh Trail ran through Laos and Cambodia, which, according to the Geneva Accords, were supposed to be neutral in any future conflicts in Vietnam. By running the trail through neutral territory, the North Vietnamese believed it would be safe from enemy attacks.

In 1960 the North Vietnamese leadership approved the creation of a multiparty political organization in the South, known as the National Liberation Front (NLF). The NLF was dominated by Vietnamese Communists, most of whom came from the North, and the North supplied much of its direction and most of its weapons and training. People came to use the informal term for the Vietnamese Communists—Viet Cong—to refer to the NLF.

CAUGHT IN A SPIRAL

There soon began a spiraling escalation of violence in Vietnam that sucked in the United States. As terror attacks increased and better-armed Viet Cong units harassed and sometimes defeated Diem's forces, the United States sent more military advisers to assist the South Vietnamese armed forces.

In 1961 U.S. military leaders recommended that the United States greatly increase its support for South Vietnam, so that South Vietnamese fighting power could match the increasing aggressiveness of NLF attacks. U.S. president John F. Kennedy approved a big increase while the NLF continued to expand its control of the South Vietnamese countryside.

The United States and the South Vietnamese government then launched the Strategic Hamlet Program. This program, modeled on a

British strategy used to defeat a Communist insurgency in Malaya, was designed to keep Viet Cong guerrillas from getting food, shelter, and recruits from the rural population of South Vietnam. The program forced farmers to move into fortified villages, built and guarded by the government. The peasants came to hate Diem's regime for moving them away from their ancestral villages. The program required yet more U.S. money, resources, and advisers but did not succeed in weakening the Viet Cong. On the contrary, the despised program brought converts to the Communists and created support for stepped-up Viet Cong attacks.

Meanwhile, in the North, the government funneled more scarce resources and men south to assist the NLF. China and the Soviet Union still supported their fellow Communists in North Vietnam. But despite substantial aid from these nations, supporting the Communist struggle in the South represented a major sacrifice for North Vietnam, which was still a very poor country.

THE END OF DIEM

As the Viet Cong gained strength, Diem's rule became increasingly unpopular. Diem lashed out at all opponents to his regime. Trying to uncover Communists, he had his security forces raid Buddhist temples. The disrespect for Buddhism, coupled with Diem's heavy-handed tactics, brought out thousands of angry protesters in Saigon. Captured by a photographer in an image that went around the world, one Buddhist monk burned himself to death to protest the Diem regime.

Another disturbing sign of things to come was the Battle of Ap Bac in early January 1963. At the town of Ap Bac, South Vietnamese army (Army of the Republic of Vietnam, or ARVN) units tried to

U.S. general Maxwell Taylor sights through a cannon on
the border of North Vietnam and South Vietnam in 1961.
At about this time, U.S. president John F. Kennedy began
sending military advisers to Vietnam to consult with the
South Vietnamese military.

trap and destroy a Viet Cong battalion. Even though the ARVN far
outnumbered the enemy and had U.S. advisers and U.S.-supplied armored personnel carriers and helicopters, the Viet Cong defeated the
ARVN units. Several helicopters and personnel carriers were lost, and
three U.S. advisers died in the battle, part of a growing toll in a war

that was getting hotter by the month. The Viet Cong victory at Ap Bac greatly encouraged leaders in the North, who in violation of the Geneva Accords, began planning to send People's Army of Vietnam (PAVN) units to overwhelm the government in the South.

The defeat at Ap Bac also made U.S. planners doubt the fighting qualities of even well-equipped ARVN units. Experts began to say that U.S. ground forces were needed to keep the South Vietnamese government from collapsing.

By 1963 the United States had around sixteen thousand advisers in South Vietnam, including a growing number of Special Forces troops (known as Green Berets) to help combat the guerrillas in the countryside. Diem, by this point, seemed less interested in fighting the Viet Cong than in making sure the ARVN would protect him and keep him in power. He also stubbornly resisted reforms the United States asked for, such as letting his political opponents take part in elections, reducing his family's corruption, and helping poor peasants.

The U.S. ambassador to South Vietnam, Henry Cabot Lodge, began scheming with South Vietnamese army generals with the goal to replace Diem through a coup, or overthrow. Taking no chances, Vietnamese plotters brutally murdered Diem and his brother on November 1, 1963.

Lodge promised to work closely with the new South Vietnamese government and continue U.S. support, but the United States found relations with the leaders who followed Diem difficult. The new leaders were generals and other military officers who had little interest in the U.S. ideals of freedom and democracy.

CHAPTER 10

Aftermath: The American War

THROUGHOUT 1964 ARVN CONTINUED to fare poorly against Viet Cong units. To bolster South Vietnamese efforts, the United States stepped up support to South Vietnam while stopping short of sending ground troops. The United States based aircraft and pilots in South Vietnam and sent more advisers and technical specialists. U.S. ships patrolled the Gulf of Tonkin.

On August 2, 1964, light North Vietnamese vessels attacked a U.S. warship off the coast of North Vietnam. The U.S. vessel returned fire. The United States claimed a second North Vietnamese attack two days later, but the evidence supporting this claim is uncertain. (Vo Nguyen Giap, who was in charge of North Vietnam's defenses at the time, admitted the first attack but denied the second.) U.S. president Lyndon Johnson responded with air strikes against North Vietnamese military facilities.

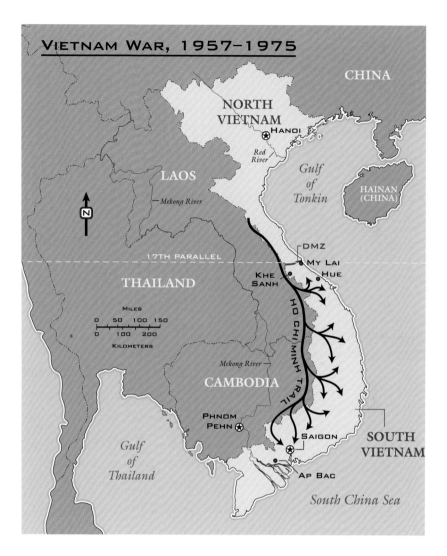

Johnson also used the attacks to persuade Congress to pass the Gulf of Tonkin Resolution. This resolution gave Johnson the power to wage war against North Vietnam, even though Congress did not formally declare war. (The United States had also fought the Korean War without a congressional declaration of war.)

In 1965 the United States committed ground forces to South Vietnam, first to protect U.S. air facilities and then to fight the increasing number of PAVN regiments coming south from North Vietnam.

The arriving Americans soon found themselves in a replay of the Indochina War that had ended a decade earlier. As the Viet Minh had done against the French, North Vietnamese and Viet Cong units refused combat or broke contact with U.S. and ARVN forces when they did not have local superiority. They retreated to hide in the jungle or in an extensive network of caves and tunnels.

IN THE MID-1960S, U.S. PRESIDENT LYNDON JOHNSON STEPPED UP U.S. INVOLVEMENT IN THE VIETNAM CONFLICT.

But U.S. troops were far better equipped than the French had been in the same situation. When U.S. ground units did engage the enemy, they could call in air support and get a speedy and massive response. Where the French had used their few helicopters mainly for medical evacuations, the United States used improved models to ferry entire units into combat.

The United States frequently carried out "search and destroy" sweeps to locate and engage Viet Cong or PAVN units and to eliminate them. Some U.S. commanders felt that in addition to engaging and destroying the enemy, the Americans had to win the "hearts and minds" of the South Vietnamese people—that is, convince them that the United States was there to help and to protect them from the Viet Cong. But the repression and corruption of the South Vietnamese government meant that many South Vietnamese never fully supported it or accepted its U.S. backers. Meanwhile, the Viet Cong continued to win converts and terrorize opponents.

A U.S. HELICOPTER FLIES OVER A HILLY JUNGLE IN VIETNAM IN 1965. U.S. FORCES USED HELICOPTERS EXTENSIVELY IN THE WAR.

Controversy

Many Americans had paid little attention to the initial buildup of U.S. advisers and other support for South Vietnam. When President Johnson decided to bomb North Vietnam in 1964 and to commit U.S. ground troops to prop up ARVN forces in 1965, many Americans backed the effort. Some agreed with air force general Curtis LeMay, who announced, "Tell the Vietnamese they've got to draw in their horns or we're going to bomb them back into the Stone Age."

But as the U.S. role in ground operations increased, along with growing U.S. casualties, some Americans began to express doubts about the war. Young men who were eligible to be drafted into the army—not eager to fight and perhaps die in a guerrilla war in the jungles of Southeast Asia—began to question U.S. involvement in Vietnam. Some Americans questioned the morality of supporting a succession of corrupt and repressive South Vietnamese regimes.

Some U.S. leaders worried that the United States had entered an unwinnable war in Vietnam. In April 1965, John McCone, director of the Central Intelligence Agency, cautioned, "I think what we are doing in starting on a track which involves ground force operations . . . [will mean] an ever-increasing commitment of U.S. personnel without materially improving the chances of victory. . . . In effect, we will find ourselves mired down in combat in the jungle in a military effort that we cannot win, and from which we will have extreme difficulty in extracting ourselves."

Starting in 1965, antiwar protests occurred on many college campuses. At first they followed the pattern of peaceful demonstration begun by the civil rights movement of the 1950s and early 1960s. Soon more radical voices emerged at protest rallies. Many decried what some saw as needless U.S. interference in other countries' affairs. Amid a general atmosphere of youth rebellion and social upheaval in the mid-1960s, antiwar demonstrations sometimes turned violent. It was not uncommon to see Viet Cong flags waved at demonstrations.

The U.S. public soon divided into antiwar "doves" and pro-war "hawks." The split occurred mainly along generational lines. Many young people were opposed to the war, while many in their parents' generation felt it was unpatriotic to speak out against the government.

THESE PROTESTERS IN PHILADELPHIA, PENNSYLVANIA, MARCH IN A DEMONSTRATION AGAINST THE WAR IN VIETNAM IN MARCH 1966. ANTIWAR PROTESTS SPRUNG UP ACROSS THE UNITED STATES IN THE 1960s.

The Trail South

As antiwar protests in the United States grew louder, the war escalated in Vietnam. North Vietnamese continued funneling supplies to the South along the Ho Chi Minh Trail. Although the trail eventually included paved sections and even fuel pipelines, much of it consisted of dirt roads. Like the Viet Minh, the North Vietnamese hauled supplies along the trail using porters, bicycles, and animals, but the North Vietnamese were also able to move much of their supplies by truck. Moving mainly at night and showing as little light as possible, drivers worked in relays. Soldiers defended key sections of the trail with antiaircraft guns.

The trail snaked through both Laos and Cambodia. In theory, both nations were neutral in the Vietnam conflict. In reality, both heavily supported the Communists. The United States was not supposed to bomb Laos or Cambodia, since they were neutral nations. So the North Vietnamese could use these neighbors as safe havens. The North Vietnamese could rest and regroup there after coming south on the Ho Chi Minh Trail or fighting across the border in South Vietnam. The North Vietnamese set up PAVN supply depots, hospitals, and even a regional headquarters inside Cambodia.

Starting in 1965, to limit the flow of supplies and weapons moving south, the United States heavily bombed sections of the trail running through Laos. But because the bombing violated Laos's neutrality, U.S. bombers carried out their raids in secret.

Turning Point: The Tet Offensive

By the end of 1967, the war in Vietnam had bogged down into a bloody stalemate. By then nearly five hundred thousand U.S. troops

John McCain in Vietnam

MANY U.S. LEADERS SERVED in Vietnam as young men. One of the most famous is John McCain, a senator and U.S. presidential candidate in 2008. McCain was a navy pilot. In 1967 his plane was shot down over North Vietnam. He endured five years of torture and brutality in a North Vietnamese prisoner-of-war camp in Hanoi. U.S. troops sarcastically dubbed the camp the Hanoi Hilton.

were serving in Vietnam, and U.S. generals were asking for more.

In early 1968, hoping to achieve a dramatic victory similar to Dien Bien Phu, the North Vietnamese tried to besiege a U.S. Marine base at Khe Sanh. The strategy involved bringing major PAVN units in from the nearby Ho Chi Minh Trail, massing them around Khe Sanh, and cutting off supplies and reinforcements to the garrison by road.

This time, however, it was the United States that held the high ground and rained death on the enemy. While the North Vietnamese were able to bring artillery and even tanks into the area, the marines had massive artillery and air support. Khe Sanh was within range of a major U.S. fire-support base (Camp Carroll). U.S.-controlled areas could be reached by road, although the PAVN blocked the main route for a time. The marines at Khe Sanh maintained a working airstrip through most of the siege, and U.S. planes brought in a far greater tonnage of supplies than had reached the French at Dien Bien Phu. After months of very heavy casualties, the North Vietnamese broke off the siege.

The fight at Khe Sanh was part of a larger campaign called the Tet Offensive, named for Tet, the Vietnamese New Year, which

A SOUTH VIETNAMESE SOLDIER WALKS THROUGH DESTRUCTION NEAR SAIGON AFTER A BATTLE DURING THE TET OFFENSIVE IN 1968.

began in 1968 on January 31. During past Tet holidays, both sides had observed informal truces and many South Vietnamese soldiers had returned home to spend the holiday with their families.

On this Tet holiday, however, Viet Cong and PAVN units attacked many of South Vietnam's cities and towns. North Vietnamese leaders saw the attacks as a General Offensive, General Uprising—the final phase in Mao's "people's war." They believed the attacks would cause the South Vietnamese people to rise up as one against the imperialist United States and its South Vietnamese puppet regime.

No Repeats

PRESIDENT LYNDON JOHNSON BECAME obsessed with avoiding a Dien Bien Phu-style defeat at the besieged U.S. combat base of Khe Sanh. Johnson told the chairman of the Joint Chiefs of Staff, "I don't want any damn Dinbinphoo."

The attacks caught U.S. and South Vietnamese forces off guard, and fighting raged throughout South Vietnam. After some initial Communist successes, U.S. and ARVN troops beat back PAVN and the Viet Cong with heavy losses. The Viet Cong military infrastructure in South Vietnam was crippled. After Tet, PAVN would do most of the fighting.

Seeking an Honorable End

For Americans back in the United States, the Vietnam conflict was the first television war. TV reporters and photographers brought the violence and brutality of the fighting into U.S. living rooms. Americans saw images of Vietnamese civilians horribly burned by napalm bombs. Americans saw terrified peasants fleeing their villages to escape advancing troops. In one horrifying incident in 1968, a group of U.S. soldiers massacred women, children, and elderly men at the South Vietnamese village of My Lai. When the incident was made public the following year, Americans reacted with outrage.

Some U.S. commanders had promised that the war was almost over, but the Tet Offensive demonstrated that the Communists were nowhere close to defeat. Meanwhile, U.S. casualties reached their peak in 1968, with more than sixteen thousand Americans killed or wounded that year.

In another replay of the French war, the United States signaled a willingness to negotiate with the Communists even as the fighting raged. The talks, held in Paris in mid-1968, stalled almost as soon as they began over questions of who could take part. The North insisted on seating the Provisional Revolutionary Government, representing the National Liberation Front, and tried to block South Vietnamese representation at the conference.

As the U.S. public tired of the war, the United States voted for a new president in 1968. The winner was Richard Nixon, a former congressman and vice president to Dwight Eisenhower. Nixon won the election partly on his promise to bring an honorable end to the conflict in Vietnam. Nixon proposed a process called Vietnamization.

U.S. PRESIDENT RICHARD NIXON DISCUSSES THE WAR IN VIETNAM DURING A PRESS CONFERENCE IN 1970.

Smoke rises as U.S. planes bomb Communist sites in Cambodia in 1970. Many Americans protested the invasion of Cambodia, which was neutral in the conflict in Vietnam.

It involved the phased withdrawal of U.S. troops as ARVN units took on more and more combat chores.

But Nixon also stepped up U.S. involvement in some areas. In 1969 he ordered a secret campaign to bomb the Ho Chi Minh Trail in Cambodia. In the spring of 1970, U.S. and ARVN units invaded Cambodia to attack North Vietnamese and Viet Cong forces operating there. With this invasion, Nixon hoped to buy time as South Vietnam's army took over more of the fighting and U.S. troops gradually withdrew.

Young Americans, angered at what they considered an unjustified escalation of the war and a violation of Cambodia's neutrality, engaged in mass protests at many U.S. universities. At Kent State University in Ohio, National Guardsmen killed four student protesters, and police in Mississippi killed two others. The deaths added to growing anger about the war and added to a split in public support for Nixon's policies. In fact, many Americans did support the war in Vietnam—they just believed it needed to be waged more forcefully.

Concern over the secrecy of the U.S. bombing campaign and the Cambodian invasion led the U.S. Congress to pass the Cooper-Church Amendment in December 1970. This law restricted U.S military operations and support for ARVN forces outside Vietnam's borders.

In the late 1960s, the U.S. military had done a secret study of U.S. involvement in Vietnam from the end of World War II to 1967. The study showed how poor decisions on the part of U.S. leaders had led the United States into war in Vietnam.

In 1971 a military analyst leaked the study, called the Pentagon Papers, to the press. The Pentagon Papers fueled further outrage against the U.S. government, especially among young Americans.

Sometimes, antiwar protesters took out their rage against soldiers returning home from Vietnam. Some veterans, who had experienced the atrocities of the Vietnam conflict firsthand, even joined the protesters. Some joined a group called Vietnam Veterans Against the War. This group questioned not only the conduct of the U.S. military during war but the reasons for fighting in Vietnam in the first place.

Talks in Paris

In the spring of 1972, ARVN showed improved fighting ability when it halted a North Vietnamese invasion across the DMZ, or demilitarized zone, the line separating North and South Vietnam at the 17th parallel. ARVN's success was due in part to massive U.S. air support, including the bombing of North Vietnam, as well as the mining of the Haiphong harbor to blow up North Vietnamese supply ships there.

The United States and North Vietnam resumed the Paris peace talks in 1972. A deal seemed close, but the talks broke down in December, and the North Vietnamese withdrew from negotiations. To force the North Vietnamese back to the table and to show support for the South Vietnamese government, President Nixon launched a massive Christmas bombing campaign against North Vietnam in December 1972. U.S. B-52 bombers pummeled Hanoi and Haiphong and destroyed much of North Vietnam's infrastructure.

The pressure worked. The North Vietnamese returned to the conference to negotiate an end to the war. The deal included a ceasefire, the return of prisoners of war, and the withdrawal of the remaining U.S. forces. The agreement also stated that the Viet Cong and South Vietnam would use negotiations and free elections to determine the future of Vietnam.

What had been accomplished after nearly two decades of U.S. involvement in Vietnam? Article I of the Paris Peace Accords reads: "The United States and all other countries respect the independence, sovereignty, unity, and territorial integrity of Viet-Nam as recognized by the 1954 Geneva Agreements on Viet-Nam." It is interesting to note that after so much destruction and so many lives lost, the situation for Vietnam, as negotiated in Paris, was no different in 1973 than it had been nineteen years earlier after the French defeat at Dien Bien Phu.

U.S. PRESIDENTIAL ADVISER HENRY KISSINGER *(RIGHT)* SHAKES HANDS WITH NORTH VIETNAMESE DELEGATE LE DUC THO DURING THE PARIS PEACE TALKS IN 1973.

Who Was First?

BY THE END OF the Vietnam War, fifty-eight thousand U.S. troops had died. Who was the first American to die in the Vietnam conflict? It depends on when you start counting. Vietnamese Communist fighters ambushed and killed U.S. Office of Strategic Services operative Peter Dewey in 1945. U.S. civilian pilots James McGovern and Wallace Bufford died at Dien Bien Phu in 1954.

The Vietnam Veterans Memorial in Washington, D.C., lists the names of all those who died between 1956 and 1975. The earliest death listed is that of air force sergeant Richard B. Fitzgibbon Jr., who died on June 8, 1956. Harry Cramer died in 1957 while training Vietnamese troops. A guerrilla attack on an air base in 1959 killed Charles Ovnand and Dale Buis. The first American killed in action was James T. Davis in December 1961.

As more Americans arrived in Vietnam, the death toll began a long climb. Among the last to die in action was marine Kelton Turner, in May 1975. He was eighteen years old when he died.

THE VIETNAM VETERANS MEMORIAL IN WASHINGTON, D.C.

Finale

A war-weary United States finally abandoned South Vietnam. By the end of 1973, the last U.S. units were gone, with only some advisers remaining. Many Americans were still angry about how President Johnson had brought the United States into the war and how he and President Nixon had conducted it. To further restrict presidential war-making powers, Congress passed the Case-Church Amendment in 1973. This law required congressional approval for further U.S. military action in Indochina. The legislation spelled the end of U.S. involvement in Vietnam.

Few expected the North Vietnamese and Viet Cong to honor the cease-fire agreed upon in Paris, and in fact, the North Vietnamese launched a major offensive in the spring of 1975. ARVN forces, no longer supplied with U.S. ammunition, soon collapsed.

The end for South Vietnam came with the fall of Saigon on April 30. It was the beginning of a Vietnam united under Communist rule.

RESIDENTS OF SAIGON TAKE TO THE STREETS TO WELCOME THE ARRIVAL OF COMMUNIST TROOPS ON APRIL 30, 1975.

To honor their leader, who had died in 1969, the Communists gave Saigon a new name: Ho Chi Minh City.

The United States improvised a massive air and sea evacuation of Americans still in Vietnam, as well as South Vietnamese civilians who did not support the new Communist government. Fearing for their lives, more than one hundred thousand South Vietnamese fled initially, with more fleeing in the following years. Many Vietnamese refugees moved to the United States, France, and other Western countries.

Many South Vietnamese who remained behind suffered greatly. The new Communist government locked up

SOUTH VIETNAMESE CIVILIANS SCRAMBLE TO GET ABOARD A U.S. AIRCRAFT DURING THE 1975 EVACUATION OF THE CITY OF NHA TRANG, ON THE COAST OF VIETNAM.

thousands of South Vietnamese in "reeducation camps." The inmates endured beatings, hunger, hard labor, and relentless Communist indoctrination. In Cambodia the Communist government imprisoned and killed people on an even larger scale.

The Legacy of the French Defeat in Vietnam

F OR MANY AMERICANS, the word *Vietnam* brings to mind the word *war*. But as the mid-twentieth century passes into memory, the Indochina War and the following Vietnam War seem more and more like old wars, to be fought in Hollywood films, television documentaries, and history books.

But the Indochina and Vietnam wars still affect the United States—in debates about current wars and foreign policy and in the experiences that have shaped our leaders. For many years after the Vietnam War, Americans were reluctant to commit troops to foreign wars. They feared a repeat of the Vietnam War, which had poorly defined goals and much public opposition—and which many thought was unwinnable. Then, in 1991, the United States fought successfully in the Persian Gulf War in the Middle Eastern nations of Kuwait and Iraq. With this victory, U.S. president George H. W. Bush announced

What's in a Name?

THE VIETNAMESE HAVE THEIR own name for the Vietnam War. It is the American War.

that Americans had finally overcome the Vietnam syndrome—the fear of being bogged down in an unwinnable foreign war.

In 2003 the United States again went to war in Iraq. This time, however, people see many parallels to the Vietnam War. They note that the United States is propping up a weak government in Iraq and fighting a guerrilla war against determined fighters with extensive civilian support. As with Vietnam, many wonder whether the Iraq war is winnable. Many Americans have also protested against the war.

POINTS OF VIEW

Americans naturally view the Vietnam War from a U.S. perspective. They think about the fifty-eight thousand young Americans killed, the 1975 collapse of the U.S.-supported South Vietnamese government, and the arrival in the United States of thousands of Vietnamese refugees. Americans also have widely different views on the Vietnam War. Some see it as a worthwhile fight for freedom. Others view it as a victory denied to U.S. forces by bungling politicians. Still others see it as an illegal and immoral war that should never have been waged.

The Vietnam War—and the preceding Indochina War—also have different meanings to the people of Southeast Asia. Entire societies in this region endured unimaginable suffering during these wars. Millions died or were wounded. Millions more were displaced from their

VIETNAMESE REFUGEES FLEE THEIR HOMES NEAR DIEN BIEN PHU IN 1954. THE INDOCHINA AND VIETNAM WARS DISPLACED MILLIONS OF VIETNAMESE.

homes. Families were torn apart as fathers, mothers, sons, and daughters fled armies and oppressive governments.

After the Vietnam War, Vietnam's new Communist government ruled oppressively. It punished its opponents and former enemies, sometimes brutalizing and murdering civilians. In the twenty-first century, Vietnam is still under Communist rule. But repression has softened. Vietnam's leaders have abandoned some of their Communist doctrine in favor of a more free-market, capitalist economy. This change has led to a growing prosperity in modern Vietnam.

Healing the Wounds of War

Estimates of the costs of the Indochina and Vietnam wars vary widely. In money terms, the price went from billions spent during the Indochina War to hundreds of billions spent during the Vietnam War. Both wars also set Vietnam back decades in terms of economic development.

The human cost is harder to tally. More than fifty thousand members of the French forces and hundreds of thousands of Vietnamese died before 1955. More than fifty-eight thousand Americans died during the Vietnam War, while hundreds of thousands more U.S. troops were badly wounded or disabled. The Vietnamese, Laotian, and Cambodian dead from the war are counted in the millions.

Under President Bill Clinton, the United States established full diplomatic relations with Vietnam in 1995. Assisting in this effort were U.S. senators John Kerry and John McCain, both Vietnam War

U.S. PRESIDENT BILL CLINTON (CENTER) SPEAKS AT A PRESS CONFERENCE ANNOUCING THE U.S. INTENTION TO NORMALIZE RELATIONS WITH VIETNAM IN 1995. SENATORS AND VIETNAM WAR VETERANS JOHN MCCAIN (TO RIGHT OF CLINTON) AND JOHN KERRY (TO LEFT OF CLINTON) HELPED IN THE EFFORT.

veterans and both unsuccessful candidates for the presidency of the United States in the early twenty-first century. The new arrangement finally brought closure to a long and difficult chapter in U.S.-Vietnamese relations that had begun fifty years earlier.

In 2002 searchers recovered the remains of James McGovern, one of the first Americans to die in the Vietnam conflict, in 1954. In 2007 McGovern was buried in Arlington National Cemetery, the nation's most revered military cemetery. His burial more than fifty years after the battle at Dien Bien Phu is evidence that memories of Vietnam still resonate in U.S. society.

The French Legacy

And what of the cherished colony that France's sons died to maintain? France's legacy in Vietnam grows fainter every year. Few modern Vietnamese learn French, once the language of all business and government in Vietnam. As modern Vietnam takes its place among the economic powers of Southeast Asia, English is the language of choice for ambitious and internationally minded young Vietnamese.

In the twenty-first century, the hellish valley of Dien Bien Phu has become home to a bustling city. Part of the battlefield is a museum run by the Vietnamese government. A small Foreign Legion memorial commemorates the site of Colonel de Castries' bunker. Above the valley, the jungle has returned to cover the roads and artillery emplacements created by the Viet Minh.

Aftermath

In the waning days of its empire after World War II, the French staked everything in an effort to maintain a presence in Indochina. The result was a struggle that reached its climax in the battle for Dien Bien Phu. The battle in that small and remote valley had a huge impact on history.

When the battle was over, a once-mighty world power had been pushed from a prized corner of its empire. New nations had been born. A different world power, the United States, tried to pick up the pieces—with results that still affect Americans more than fifty years later.

Timeline

207 B.C.	The Chinese take control of Vietnam.
A.D. 939	The Vietnamese revolt against Chinese rule and create their own government.
1407	China's Ming dynasty takes over Vietnam.
1428	After ousting the Chinese, Le Loi becomes emperor of Vietnam.
1516	Portuguese traders arrive in Vietnam.
1619	Alexandre de Rhodes, a French missionary, arrives in Vietnam.
1772	Rebels from the Tay Son region take control in Vietnam.
1802	Nguyen Anh defeats the Tay Son rebels and declares himself emperor of Vietnam.
1847	Angered by the persecution of French missionaries and Vietnamese Catholics, French ships shell Da Nang.
1851	Emperor Tu Duc orders a crackdown on Vietnamese Catholics and foreign priests.
1858	French forces invade Da Nang.
1862	Emperor Tu Duc signs a treaty giving France control of Cochin China.
1883	France establishes control over all Vietnam.
1911	Ho Chi Minh leaves Vietnam for the West.
1920	Ho Chi Minh joins the French Communist Party.

1930	Ho Chi Minh creates the Vietnamese Communist Party. Vietnamese nationalists revolt against French rule, and Vietnamese peasants revolt against their landlords. The French crush both revolts.
1939	World War II begins in Europe.
1940	Germany invades France and sets up the German-controlled Vichy government.
1941	Ho Chi Minh forms the Viet Nam Doc Lap Dong Minh Hoi, called Viet Minh for short. Japan attacks Pearl Harbor, Hawaii, bringing the United States into World War II.
1945	World War II ends. Ho Chi Minh declares the creation of the Democratic Republic of Vietnam. The French try to reestablish control in Vietnam.
1946	Vietnam becomes a member of the Indochinese Federation. Ho Chi Minh signs the Fontainebleau Agreement, giving France significant control in Vietnam. French and Viet Minh forces clash at Haiphong and Hanoi. The Indochina War begins.
1949	France creates the Associated State of Vietnam, headed by Bao Dai, the former Vietnamese emperor.
1950	China and the Soviet Union recognize the Viet Minh as the legitimate government of Vietnam. North Korea invades South Korea, starting the Korean War.
1952	Using the "hedgehog" technique, the French defeat the Viet Minh at Na San.
1953	The Korean War ends in a stalemate. General Henri Navarre plans Operation Castor and moves troops to Dien Bien Phu. The Viet Minh also move troops to Dien Bien Phu.

1954	The Viet Minh defeat the French at Dien Bien Phu. The Geneva Accords establish Vietnam as an independent nation, with its government to be determined by future elections.
1955	Ngo Dinh Diem takes over in South Vietnam. U.S. military and civilian advisers arrive to assist the South Vietnamese government.
1956	The last French troops leave Vietnam.
1957	Viet Cong guerrillas begin a terror campaign in South Vietnam.
1959	The North Vietnamese begin building a supply route (the Ho Chi Minh Trail) to send weapons and equipment to Viet Cong fighters in the South.
1960	The North Vietnamese create the National Liberation Front.
1961	The United States increases its support for South Vietnam.
1963	The Viet Cong defeat ARVN units at the Battle of Ap Bac. Military leaders kill Ngo Dinh Diem and his brother and take over the South Vietnamese government.
1964	Vietnamese ships attack a U.S. warship in the Gulf of Tonkin. The United States bombs North Vietnamese military facilities. The U.S. Congress passes the Gulf of Tonkin Resolution, allowing President Lyndon Johnson to wage war against North Vietnam.
1965	The first U.S. ground forces arrive in Vietnam. Americans hold antiwar protests on college campuses.
1968	The North Vietnamese launch the Tet Offensive in South Vietnamese cities and towns. U.S. soldiers massacre civilians in the village of My Lai. Peace talks begin in Paris.

1969	The United States bombs the Ho Chi Minh Trail in Cambodia.
1970	The United States and South Vietnamese troops invade Cambodia.
1971	Newspapers print the Pentagon Papers, which reveal poor U.S. decision making leading to the Vietnam War.
1972	The Paris peace talks resume. The United States launches a "Christmas bombing" campaign against North Vietnam.
1973	The Paris Peace Accords list terms for an end to the Vietnam War. The United States pulls its last troops out of Vietnam.
1975	Saigon falls to the North Vietnamese. The United States evacuates thousands of South Vietnamese civilians.
1995	The United States establishes full diplomatic relations with Vietnam.

Glossary

camouflage: the disguising of soldiers and military equipment with paint, nets, or foliage

capitalism: an economic system based on the private ownership of goods and property, free enterprise, and business competition

casualty: the loss of military personnel in wartime due to death, injury, illness, or capture

colonialism: the policy or practice by which one country sends settlers to another country and establishes political control there

column: a long row of soldiers and military equipment

Communism: a political and economic system in which the government controls all business, property, and economic activity in a nation

guerrilla warfare: warfare conducted by small bands of fighters, using tactics such as ambushes, raids, and bombings

insurrection: the act of revolting against the established government

Marxism: the political, economic, and social principles espoused by German philosophers Karl Marx and Friedrich Engels and that form the basis for Communist philosophy

missionary: a religious teacher who tries to convert others to his or her faith

nationalism: loyalty to one's nation, pride in its history and culture, and a desire for national independence

occupation: the holding and control of an area by a foreign military force

propaganda: ideas, information, or rumors spread to promote a cause, person, or group

protectorate: a nation under the protection and partial control of another nation

refugee: a person who flees his or her country to find safety elsewhere

siege: a military tactic in which an army surrounds a town or military installation and keeps food, water, weapons, and other supplies from reaching the people inside

Western: relating to the democratic, industrialized nations of Western Europe and North America

Who's Who?

Bao Dai (1913–1997): Bao Dai was the last emperor of the Nguyen dynasty—although he ruled as only a figurehead under French control. The Japanese put him at the head of a puppet government at the end of World War II. The French also placed him at the head of puppet governments during the Indochina War. Ngo Dinh Diem removed Bao Dai from his position as head of the Associated State of Vietnam in 1955. He went into exile in France, where he lived until his death.

Charles de Gaulle (1890–1970): General and leader of the Free French during World War II, de Gaulle headed the postwar French government and directed the French return to Indochina. He resigned his office in 1946 but returned in 1958 to lead France during the Algerian crisis. He remained president of France until 1968.

Ngo Dinh Diem (1901–1963): The Catholic, anti-Communist Diem was a close ally of the United States and had met many influential U.S. leaders. Thanks to a rigged election in 1955, Diem became the first president of the Republic of Vietnam, or South Vietnam. Diem was popular at first, but his government soon became corrupt and repressive. The United States favored a change of government for South Vietnam, and Diem's own generals murdered him and his brother in 1963.

John Foster Dulles (1888–1959): A prominent U.S. politician, Dulles was fiercely anti-Communist. He became U.S. secretary of state in 1953. During the Indochina War, Dulles wanted strong U.S. support for the French in Vietnam. In 1954 Dulles made sure that the United States did not sign the Geneva Accords, which he believed would open the door for a Communist government in Vietnam. Dulles served as secretary of state until his death in 1959.

Dwight D. Eisenhower (1890–1969): Eisenhower served in World War II as the leader of the Allied forces in Europe. He served two terms as U.S. president, from 1953 to 1961. Eisenhower was cautious about direct U.S. military intervention in Vietnam, but he supported sending aid to France and later to Ngo Dinh Diem to oppose the spread of Communism in Southeast Asia.

Vo Nguyen Giap (1912–): A teacher with no formal military training, Giap built the Viet Minh forces from a small band of fighters into the multidivision force that defeated the French at Dien Bien Phu. Giap went on to direct the North Vietnamese against South Vietnam and the United States during the Vietnam War. He is considered one of the greatest military strategists of the twentieth century.

Ho Chi Minh (1890–1969): Ho Chi Minh was a well-traveled student and teacher of Communist revolutionary doctrine and a dedicated Vietnamese nationalist. He founded the Communist-dominated Viet Minh movement in 1941 and became president of the Democratic Republic of Vietnam in 1945. During the Indochina War, Ho directed the struggles of the Viet Minh against France. He later led North Vietnam and the Viet Cong in their war against South Vietnam and the United States. He died in 1969. Ho Chi Minh City (formerly Saigon) is named in his honor.

Lyndon B. Johnson (1908–1973): Johnson served as a U.S. senator and as vice president of the United States under John F. Kennedy. When Kennedy was assassinated, Johnson became president. He began direct U.S. involvement in Vietnam with the Gulf of Tonkin Resolution in 1964. He oversaw a massive buildup of U.S. troops in South Vietnam as well as a prolonged bombing campaign in the North. Frustrated with the war's progress and with antiwar protests, Johnson decided in 1968 not to seek reelection to the presidency.

Mao Zedong (1893–1976): Mao helped found the Chinese Communist Party in 1921. He developed the doctrine of a "people's war" fought by a "people's army." His ideas greatly influenced the Communists in Vietnam, including Ho Chi Minh. Mao sent weapons, supplies, and advisers to aid the Viet Minh during the Indochina War. He led China until his death in 1976.

Henri Navarre (1898–1983): Navarre was the French commander in Indochina in 1953 and 1954. He devised a plan to lure Viet Minh forces to their destruction at Dien Bien Phu. The plan backfired, and the French ended up defeated there. Navarre retired from the French military in 1956.

Richard Nixon (1913–1994): Nixon served as a congressman, senator, and vice president of the United States before winning the presidency in 1968. He instituted a policy of Vietnamization, which involved withdrawing U.S. troops from Vietnam and letting ARVN take over the fighting. He also oversaw the illegal bombing and invasion of Cambodia in 1969 and 1970. Nixon resigned his office after the 1973 Watergate scandal, which involved illegal activities on the part of his staff.

Pierre Pigneau de Béhaine (1741–1799): A French missionary, Pigneau traveled to Vietnam in 1765. He trained Asian priests on an island off the coast of Vietnam. In 1777 Prince Nguyen Anh fled to the island and met Pigneau. He arranged for French military aid to help Nguyen Anh become emperor of a united Vietnam.

Alexandre de Rhodes (1591–1660): Rhodes was a French Catholic missionary and scholar. He worked in Vietnam between 1620 and 1649. During this time, he helped create the modern Vietnamese alphabet. Rhodes wrote about his work in Vietnam, and his writings created increased French interest in Vietnam.

Source Notes

18 Paul Halsall, ed., "Jules Ferry (1832–1893): On French Colonial Expansion," *Internet Modern History Sourcebook*, 1998, http://www.fordham.edu/halsall/mod/1884ferry.html (November 21, 2008).

21 V. I. Lenin, "Imperialism and the Split in Socialism," *Marxists Internet Archive*, 2008, http://www.marxists.org/archive/lenin/works/1916/oct/x01.htm (November 21, 2008).

29 Stanley Karnow, *Vietnam: A History* (New York: Viking Press, 1983), 139.

31 International Relations Department, Mount Holyoke College, ed., "Background to the Crisis," *The Pentagon Papers*, 1971, http://www.mtholyoke.edu/acad/intrel/pentagon/pent1.html (November 21, 2008).

46 Stanley Karnow, "Giap Remembers," *New York Times*, June 24, 1990, http://query.nytimes.com/gst/fullpage.html?res=9C0CE1D8163AF937A15755C0A966958260&sec=&spon=&pagewanted=all (November 3, 2008).

89 Matrix, "Domino Theory Principle, Dwight D. Eisenhower, 1954," *Michigan State University*, 2008, http://coursesa.matrix.msu.edu/~hst306/documents/domino.html (October 30, 2008).

120 "Vietnam War Quotes," *The Patriot Files*, 2008, http://www.patriotfiles.com/forum/showthread.php?t=37971 (November 3, 2008).

120 CIA, "1963–1965: CIA Judgments on President Johnson's Decision to 'Go Big' in Vietnam," *Central Intelligence Agency*, 2007, https://www.cia.gov/library/center-for-the-study-of-intelligence/csi-publications/books-and-monographs/cia-and-the-vietnam-policymakers-three-episodes-1962-1968/epis2.html (November 21, 2008).

125 "Airlift's Role at Dien Bien Phu and Khe Sanh," *Global Security.org*, 1991, http://www.globalsecurity.org/military/library/report/1991/ FRF.htm (November 2008).

129 Ashbrook Center for Public Affairs, "The Paris Accords," *Teaching American History.org*, 2008, http://www.teachingamericanhistory .org/library/index.asp?document=726 (November 21, 2008).

Selected Bibliography

Arnold, James. *First Domino: Eisenhower, the Military, and America's Intervention in Vietnam.* New York: William Morrow, 1991.

Cable, James. *The Geneva Conference of 1954 on Indochina.* New York: St. Martin's, 1986.

Camus, Daniel, and Jules Roy. *Dien Bien Phu.* Paris: Julliard, 1963.

Currey, Cecil. *Victory at Any Cost: The Genius of Vietnam's General Giap.* New York: Brassey's, 1996.

Doyle, Edward, Samuel Lipsman, and the editors of Boston Publishing Company. *Setting the Stage.* Boston: Boston Publishing Company, 1981.

Doyle, Edward, Samuel Lipsman, Stephen Weiss, and the editors of Boston Publishing Company. *America Takes Over, 1965–67.* Boston: Boston Publishing Company, 1982.

———. *Passing the Torch.* Boston: Boston Publishing Company, 1981.

Drez, Ronald J., and Douglas Brinkley. *Voices of Courage: The Battle for Khe Sanh, Vietnam.* New York: Bulfinch Press, 2005.

Fall, Bernard B. *Hell in a Very Small Place.* Cambridge, MA: Da Capo Press, 2002.

———. *Street without Joy.* New York: Schocken Books, 1972.

Fischer, Julene, Robert Stone, and the editors of Boston Publishing Company. *Images of War.* Boston: Boston Publishing Company, 1986.

Giap, Vo Nguyen. *Once Again We Will Win.* Hanoi: Foreign Languages Publishing House, 1966.

———. *People's War, People's Army.* New York: Praeger, 1962.

Lacouture, Jean. *Ho Chi Minh.* Translated by Peter Wiles. New York: Random House, 1968.

Lawrence, Mark Atwood. *Assuming the Burden: Europe and the American Commitment to War in Vietnam.* Berkeley: University of California Press, 2005.

Prados, John. *The Sky Would Fall: Operation Vulture: The U.S. Bombing Mission in Indochina, 1954.* New York: Dial Press, 1983.

Roy, Jules. *The Battle of Dien Bien Phu.* 2nd ed. New York: Carroll and Graf, 2002.

Ruane, Kevin. *The Vietnam Wars.* Manchester, UK: Manchester University Press, 2000.

Sagar, D. J. *Major Political Events in Indo-China 1945–1990.* New York: Facts on File, 1991.

Sheehan, Neil, and others. *The Pentagon Papers.* New York: Bantam, 1971.

———. *Tiger in the Barbed Wire: An American in Vietnam: 1952–1991.* Washington, DC: Brassey's, 1992.

Windrow, Martin. *The French Indochina War 1946–54.* New York: Osprey Publishing, 1998.

———. *The Last Valley: Dien Bien Phu and the French Defeat in Vietnam.* Cambridge, MA: Da Capo Press, 2004.

Wintle, Justin. *The Viet Nam Wars.* New York: St. Martin's, 1991.

Further Reading and Websites

BOOKS

Levy, Debbie. *Lyndon Johnson*. Twenty-First Century Books, 2003. Shortly after becoming president in 1964, Lyndon Johnson ramped up U.S. involvement in Vietnam to new levels. This book explores Johnson's life, presidency, and legacy.

———. *The Vietnam War*. Twenty-First Century Books, 2004. This fact-filled title details the soldiers, the leaders, and the nations who fought in Vietnam, as well as the battles, the equipment, and situations on the home front.

Sherman, Josepha. *The Cold War*. Twenty-First Century Books, 2004. The Indochina War and the Vietnam War were both part of the Cold War—a larger struggle between the Communist Soviet Union and the anti-Communist United States. This book examines all facets of that war.

Simpson, Howard R. *Dien Bien Phu: The Epic Battle America Forgot*. Washington, DC: Potomac Books, 2005. This young adult title focuses specifically on the battle at Dien Bien Phu and offers extensive facts and analysis.

Taus-Bolstad, Stacy. *Vietnam in Pictures*. Twenty-First Century Books, 2005. The title offers a thorough look at the nation of Vietnam, from its geography to its history to its people and culture.

Worth, Richard. *Dien Bien Phu*. Philadelphia: Chelsea House Publications, 2003. Worth explains the long struggle between the French and the Vietnamese and its culmination at Dien Bien Phu.

FILMS

Battlefield Vietnam: Dien Bien Phu the Legacy. VHS. Alexandria, VA: Time-Life Video, 1998. This film provides a good overview of the Indochina War and the Battle of Dien Bien Phu.

Battle for Dien Bien Phu. DVD. Newton, NJ: Shanachie Entertainment, 2005. This film employs historical footage, interviews, and solid narration to tell the story of the Battle of Dien Bien Phu.

WEBSITES

Battlefield Vietnam: PBS
http://www.pbs.org/battlefieldvietnam/index.html
This website is a companion to the outstanding PBS television series on the Indochina and Vietnam wars.

Vietnam Online
http://www.pbs.org/wgbh/amex/vietnam/series/index.html
This website accompanies *Vietnam: A Television History*, part of the acclaimed *American Experience* series.

Vietnam Veterans Memorial
http://thewall-usa.com/names.asp
The Vietnam Veterans Memorial in Washington, D.C., is a stark black granite wall inscribed with the names of the more than fifty-eight thousand Americans who died in Vietnam. This website offers extensive information on the wall and allows you to search for specific names.

Visual Geography Series
http://www.vgsbooks.com
Visit vgsbooks.com, the home page of the Visual Geography Series®, which is updated regularly. You can get linked to all sorts of useful online information, including geographical, historical, demographic, cultural, and economic websites. The vgsbooks.com site is a great resource for late-breaking news and statistics about a variety of nations, including Vietnam.

Index

Photo Acknowledgments

The images in this book are used with the permission of: AP Photo, pp. 5, 36, 50, 54, 78, 88, 92, 108, 114, 133; © Laura Westlund/Independent Picture Service, pp. 7, 49, 117; © Mary Evans Picture Library/The Image Works, p. 11; © Roger-Viollet/ The Image Works, pp. 15, 17, 27; © AFP/Getty Images, pp. 21, 37, 59, 69, 90, 99, 111, 132; © FIA/RDA/Hulton Archive/Getty Images, p. 23; © Laure Albin-Guillot/ Roger-Viollet/The Image Works, p. 33; © Jack Birns/Time Life Pictures/Getty Images, p. 39; National Archives, p. 42; © Bettmann/CORBIS, pp. 53, 56, 61, 127; © Joseph Scherschel/Time Life Pictures/Getty Images, p. 66; © Hulton Archive/Getty Images, p. 68; © Keystone Pictures/ZUMA Press, pp. 71, 97, 136; © STAFF/AFP/Getty Images, pp. 72, 84; © CORBIS, p. 73; © Topham/The Image Works, p. 83; Library of Congress, pp. 94 (LC-USZ62-104961), 118 (LC-USZ62-13036); AP-Photo/mn/ stf, p. 102; © Howard Sochurek/Time Life Pictures/Getty Images, p. 104; © Rolls Press/Popperfoto/Getty Images, p. 119; AP Photo/Bill Ingraham, p. 121; AP Photo/ Nick Ut, p. 124; © STF/AFP/Getty Images, p. 126; AP Photo/Michel Lipchitz, p. 130; © Ken Cole/Dreamstime.com, p. 131; © Diana Walker/Time Life Pictures/ Getty Images, p. 137.

Cover: AP Photo.

About the Authors

Mark E. Cunningham majored in history and political science at the University of Iowa and received an MA in English as a second language at the University of Northern Arizona. A former Peace Corps volunteer, he has lived and worked all over the world. Cunningham teaches at Michigan State University.

Lawrence J. Zwier is the associate director of the English Language Center at Michigan State University. He wrote *The Persian Gulf and Iraq Wars.*